Steel in the 21st Century

Competition Forges a New World Order

William T. Hogan, S.J.

LEXINGTON BOOKS
An Imprint of Macmillan, Inc.
NEW YORK

Maxwell Macmillan Canada
TORONTO

Maxwell Macmillan International
NEW YORK   OXFORD   SINGAPORE   SYDNEY

Library of Congress Cataloging-in-Publication Data

Hogan, William Thomas.
    Steel in the 21st century : competition forges a new world order /
William T. Hogan.
        p.   cm.
    Includes index.
    ISBN 0-02-914795-6
    1. Steel industry and trade—Forecasting.   2. Competition.
International.   3. Twenty-first century—Forecasts.   I. Title.
II. Title: Steel in the twenty-first century.
    HD9510.5.H569   1994
    338.4'7669142'021—dc20   94-10301
                                                              CIP

Lexington Books
An Imprint of Macmillan, Inc.
866 Third Avenue, New York, N.Y. 10022

Maxwell Macmillan Canada, Inc.
1200 Eglinton Avenue East
Suite 200
Don Mills, Ontario M3C 3N1

Macmillan, Inc. is part of the Maxwell Communication Group of Companies.

Printed in the United States of America

printing number
1   2   3   4   5   6   7   8   9   10

Contents

Preface   v

1   Competitive Forces Reshaping Steel   1

2   Industrialized versus Developing Countries   7

3   Minimills versus Integrated Mills   74

4   Substitute Materials   120

5   The Steel Mill of the 21st Century   138

6   Summary   183

Notes   187
Bibliography   188
Index   192
About the Author   201

Preface

The world steel industry has long been divided into three segments; the industrialized nations, which include the United States, Canada, Japan, and the countries of Western Europe; the developing countries, which include most of the African and Asian countries, as well as those in Latin America; and the former countries of the Communist bloc, which was constituted by the Soviet Union and a number of countries in Eastern Europe. This no longer exists and is undergoing considerable change as well as reduction in size.

The developing countries now have increased their steel production significantly. Between 1980 and 1992, their output more than doubled, from 102 million tonnes to 214 million tonnes. Most of these countries have plans for growth during the remainder of the 1990s and on into the 21st century. The industrialized countries, on the other hand, if anything will reduce their capacity in the years ahead. Whatever growth will be experienced there will come from the installation of minimills.

There has been considerable advance in technology, particularly in regard to the iron and steelmaking segments of the industry. The most significant developments are covered in chapter 5 on technology.

The steel industry in Western Europe, particularly in Germany and Italy, is in a state of flux. Consequently, there could be changes while the book is still in press.

Sources for this book consist principally of interviews with top management steel personnel on a global basis, as well as information drawn from the American Iron and Steel Institute, the International Iron and Steel Institute, the Japan Iron and Steel Federation, *Metal Bulletin,* and *American Metal Market.* The statistics are presented in both metric and net tons and can be identified by the spelling. *Tons* indicates net tons and *tonnes* indicates metric tonnes.

The author wishes particularly to thank Frank T. Koelble, a long-time associate at the Industrial Economics Research Institute, Fordham University, for significant and valuable contributions to this book.

1
Competitive Forces Reshaping Steel

As a "new world order" struggles to emerge in the aftermath of the cold war, the world steel industry remains in the throes of its own upheaval, driven by powerful competitive forces that are forging drastic changes in one of the most basic of all manufacturing industries. Steelmakers, in fact, are locked in a protracted competitive struggle, one that will ultimately determine just where steel is to be made, by what companies, and in what quantities. In the process, a new, twenty-first century steel industry will emerge, composed of steel companies transformed in their most essential characteristics as to structure, technology, production, and marketing.

The steel industry in the twenty-first century will be significantly changed from the industry that existed in the 1980s. The developing countries will increase their share of steel production, while the industrialized countries will reduce production. Total world steel capacity for the early part of the twenty-first century will be in the area of 800–850 million tonnes.

The steel industry in the post–World War II period has experienced a number of dramatic developments. From the end of the war in 1945 to 1974, it had virtually continual growth in capacity as well as production. World capacity grew from 135 million tonnes to over 700 million tonnes between 1947 and 1974. In 1974, a record production year, optimism was strong and projections were made to increase capacity by 240 million

1

tonnes with virtually the entire world participating, as table 1–1 indicates.

In the years immediately following 1974, however, a recession was experienced by the steel industry worldwide. Between 1974 and 1975 Japanese steel production fell by 14 percent. The European Community (EC) output declined by 19 percent, and that of the United States by 20 percent. The next few years witnessed a recession and the 240 million tonnes of projected increased capacity failed to materialize. This recession was caused, in part, by the oil shock that disrupted the economies of a number of countries, particularly those that depended heavily on oil imports. The price of a barrel of oil rose from less than $3 to almost $12 in the space of one year. This increase absorbed the cash and capital of many countries that had to import oil, and as a consequence the steel industry in those areas did not realize the expansion that had been projected.

There was somewhat of a recovery in the late 1970s. By 1980 steel industry output had improved from the decline in the mid-1970s to a figure of 716 million tonnes. However, there was another decline in 1982, this one particularly severe, as world steel output fell to 645 million tonnes. In the United States, output dropped from 120 million tons in 1978 to 74 million tons in 1982, a precipitous decline.

In the subsequent years steel production gradually improved,

Table 1–1
Additional Steel Capacity Projections By Regions, 1974–85
(*million metric tons*)

EEC of 9	41.3
Other Western Europe	26.7
North America	28.5
Latin America	37.2
Africa	12.3
Middle East	23.8
Far East	67.9
Oceania	2.3
Total	240.0

so that by 1989 a worldwide record of 786 million tonnes was established. But by 1992 production declined to 714 million tonnes. Thus, the industry in the postwar period followed a cyclical trend in terms of output.

It must be stated, however, that the increase in the use of continuous casting—to 95 percent in Japan, 90 percent in the EC, and 80 percent in the United States—improved the yield because fewer tonnes of crude steel are required to produce the same amount of finished products. Further, the industry has developed lighter steels, whose production contributed to the decline in tonnage of crude steel. Moreover, the steel consumers, through improvements in their production processes, increased the yield of the finished products from steel or conversely decreased scrap loss, thereby requiring less steel. In the automobile industry, the scrap loss in steel declined considerably.

In terms of geographic location, there was a notable shift in steel production during the postwar period. In the early years of the 1950s the developing countries produced very little steel. In 1975, a at a conference held in Lima, Peru, the developing countries set their sights on increasing their steel output to 25–30 percent of world output by the year 2000. The Conference members noted that the developing countries had 70 percent of the world's population, but only 7 percent of the world's industrial production. This was to be rectified by the year 2000 to a point where industrial output in the developing countries would be 25 percent of total worldwide production. The possibility of achieving this ratio in steel was very much in doubt, particularly since projections made in 1975 for world steel output by 2000 placed it between 1.4 billion and 1.75 billion tonnes, 25 percent of which would be approximately 350 to about 440 million tonnes. This target seemed to be beyond reach. However, significant growth in steel tonnage in developing countries as well as a reduction in the projected tonnage will make it possible for the 25 percent figure to be realized by the developing countries. In 1980 these countries produced 102 million tonnes, and by 1992 they were producing 214 million tonnes. By the year 2000, output for the developing countries could reach 250 million tonnes. Since projections for that year for total world output have been scaled down to 800–850 million tonnes, the 250-tonne output for the developing countries would be well over 25 percent of the world total. In fact, in 1992, with an output of 214 million tonnes out of a total of 714 million, the developing countries accounted for some 29 percent of world steel output.

Significant growth is projected for a number of developing countries, particularly the People's Republic of China. Meanwhile, the industrialized nations have reduced their steelmaking capacity by 100 million tonnes from the mid-1970s to 1990. Since the output of the developing countries continues to expand, and that of the industrialized countries continues to contract, there is little doubt that developing countries will produce more than 30 percent of world steel by the year 2000.

In the past twenty years the steel industry has witnessed a growth in three new types of competition. The first is the competition between the industrialized countries and the developing countries. This has taken place in the past twenty years and has grown considerably during the 1980s. In 1980, third world production was 102 million tonnes versus 440 million for the industrialized countries. By 1992 this situation had changed dramatically as the production of developing countries increased to 214 million tonnes while the output of the industrialized countries fell to 359 million tonnes. This was a result of an increase in third world capacity and production and almost a corresponding decrease in capacity and production in the industrialized countries.

The second form of competition concerns methods of production between minimills versus integrated mills. This development was achieved in two stages. In the first stage, minimills moved into the production of products such as concrete reinforcing bars and light structurals, including channels, angles, and bars. After a period of approximately ten years, the integrated mills in the United States abandoned these products, so that they became the complete province of the minimills. This was not unforeseen or unusual, since these products were not particularly profitable for the integrated companies. Since 1988, with the introduction of the thin-slab caster, minimills have begun to produce flat-rolled products. This was an innovation, since the electric furnace and the small rolling mill were never considered a logical entrance into flat products. However, this has been achieved in a few instances in the United States as well as in Europe and Japan, and it appears that more such mills will be constructed in the remainder of the twentieth century, so that minimills could be producing as much as 8–10 percent of the sheet steel product by the turn of the century. This is revolutionary insofar as minimills were never thought of as sheet producers before the closing years of the 1980s. The competition between the minimills and the integrated mills has expanded beyond the sheet business to heavy structurals, where in the United States, three companies, namely, Nucor in a joint venture with Yamato of Japan, Chapparel by itself, and Northwestern Steel & Wire, dominate the heavy structural, wide flange beam market.

The third type of competition has been between steel products and substitute nonsteel products. For example, reinforced concrete began to be used to replace structural steel after World War II, at a time when structural steel was in short supply. Since that time, substitution has spread to ceramics, which are often used instead of cast iron for application in areas where considerable heat is generated. Aluminum has taken the place of tinplate in the beverage and beer can business, and now accounts for 96 percent of that market in the United States, but less in Japan and the EC. In the automobile industry, aluminum use has increased since 1980, when it constituted 130 pounds per vehicle, to 177 pounds per vehicle by 1993. Plastics use also grew from 196 pounds per vehicle to 243 pounds. This is in contrast to steel which in 1980 was 1893.5 pounds per vehicle as compared with 1726.4 pounds in 1993. The decline was not due to a replacement as much as to the fact that less steel and lighter steels are being used.

The three phases of competition in which steel is engaged have resulted in additional capital expenditures as well as increased and improved research programs on the part of the steel industry.

2
Industrialized versus Developing Countries

General Industry Trends

The steel industry on a worldwide basis has been divided into three groups: the industrialized countries, the developing countries, and up until 1989, the Communist bloc, consisting of the Soviet Union and several Eastern European countries. Total world production of steel in 1992 was 714 million tonnes: 359 million tonnes for the industrialized countries, 214 million tonnes for the developing countries, and 141 million tonnes for the former Communist bloc. This chapter will discuss the growth of the worldwide steel industry over a period of years as well as the decline of certain of its segments. It will also discuss the competition between the industrialized and developing countries, and prospects for individual steel-producing countries.

Since 1974 there has been a decided growth in the amount of steel produced by developing countries. This growth contrasts with somewhat declining output in the industrialized countries from 1980 through 1992. In 1980 the total steel produced by industrialized countries was 440 million tonnes. This output declined to 359 million tonnes in 1992. Meanwhile, in 1980, the developing countries produced a total of 102 million tonnes, and by 1992 were producing 214 million tonnes. Obviously, the growth in the steel industry since 1980 has taken place in the developing countries, led by the People's Republic of China

7

which over the last twelve years has increased its output from 37 million tonnes to 80 million tonnes. Other developing countries have also increased their output since 1974, as table 2–1 indicates. Table 2–1 lists steel production figures for 1974, 1980, and 1992 for twelve developing countries and indicates a very significant growth in output for all countries except Argentina.

The condition of the industrialized countries in terms of steel production between 1974 and 1992 is illustrated in table 2–2. Of the nine countries listed, only three, Italy, Canada, and Spain, have been able to maintain their 1974 levels of output. The output for the other six countries has declined, in some cases relatively slightly and in others drastically.

The steel industry in the industrialized countries has also witnessed a sharp decline in employment between 1974 and 1992 as table 2–3 indicates.

Growth in the developing countries has brought them into a position to compete with the industrialized countries to a significant extent. In fact, they now produce 29 percent of the world's total steel output, which surpasses the goal announced at the 1975 Lima Conference for Developing Countries. This growth contrasts with the decline in the industrialized countries and has led to significant competition between the two groups.

Table 2–1
Third World Steel Production for 1974, 1980, and 1992
(thousands of tonnes)

	1974	1980	1992
China	21,119	37,121	80,037
Brazil	7,515	15,309	23,898
South Korea	1,947	8,558	28,054
India	7,069	9,514	18,117
Taiwan	597	3,417	10,705
Mexico	5,138	7,156	8,436
Argentina	2,353	2,687	2,661
Venezuela	1,058	1,975	3,396
Turkey	1,590	2,536	10,254
Saudi Arabia	—	—	1,823
Iran	567	1,200	2,937
Egypt	500	800	1,400

Table 2–2
Industrialized Countries' Steel Production for 1974, 1980, and 1992
(thousands of tonnes)

	1974	1980	1992
United States	136,802[a]	101,455	84,322
Japan	119,322[a]	111,395	98,132
Germany	53,232	43,838	38,711[b]
United Kingdom	26,594[a]	11,227	16,050
France	27,021	23,176	17,961
Italy	23,804	26,501	24,904
Spain	11,502	12,643	12,295
Belgium	16,227	12,322	10,330
Canada	13,623	15,901	13,933

[a] Production in 1973.
[b] Includes former East Germany.

This is manifested particularly in the export market. As early as 1981 an item in the *Japanese Economic Journal* stated:

> Steel exports this year are likely to dip below the initially estimated 30 million tonne level, probably to around 29 million tonnes. This is because steel exports are being confronted with lower priced products from South Korea, Eastern European countries, and South Africa in the southeast Asian market. They are also fiercely competing with their European counterparts and the United States, Canada,

Table 2–3
Employment in the Steel Industry
(in thousands)

	1974	1992
Belgium	64	25
France	158	43
Germany	232	132
Italy	96	50
Spain	89	33
United Kingdom	194	41
Canada	77	51
United States	521	190
Japan	459	304

Source: International Iron and Steel Institute, *1993 World Steel in Figures.*

Note: By contrast, India increased its employment between 1974 and 1992 from 97,000 to 294,000.

and for South American and Middle Eastern markets. . . . According to major steel firms, staffers in charge of exports, their contracts with southeast Asian countries have begun to slacken mainly because Pohang Iron and Steel Company, South Korea's largest steelmaker, has begun to export its hot coils at prices 4 to 5 percent lower than that of Japanese counterparts.

Pohang Iron and Steel's full-fledged hot coil supply also is expected to bring down Japan's hot coil exports to South Korea to around 400,000 tonnes this year from 1 million tonnes in the past.[1]

Japanese exports declined dramatically from a high point of 36 million tonnes in 1976 to the current level of approximately 19 million tonnes. A substantial drop took place between 1981 and 1992, when exports plummeted from 29.1 million tonnes to 18 million tonnes.

Several developing countries have so increased their own steel output that they no longer need large quantities of Japanese steel imports. For example, Japanese steel exports to Iran declined from 501,000 tonnes in 1981 to 267,000 tonnes in 1991, a drop of nearly half. This drop was the direct result of an increase in Iran's steel production from 565,000 tonnes in 1981 to 1,425,000 tonnes in 1990. Likewise, Saudi Arabia imported 1,842,000 tonnes of steel from Japan in 1981, but with the development of the steel industry in that country, Japanese imports fell to 486,000 tonnes in 1991, while Saudi Arabia's steel production rose from virtually nothing in 1981 to 1.8 million tonnes in 1990.

South Korea provides a good example of competition between a developing country and Japan in the export market. In 1986 Japan exported 10 million tonnes of steel to China, but by 1992 it exported only 2.4 million tonnes. Meanwhile, South Korea increased its exports to China from 300,000 tonnes in 1988 to 2.1 million tonnes in 1992. The drop in Japanese exports is due in part to the growth of steel production within China. South Korea has managed to secure a significant part of the Chinese market.

Significantly, the People's Republic of China increased its

steel exports from 150,000 tonnes in the mid-1980s to 3 million tonnes in 1992. This growth in exports reflects growth in domestic steel production, which rose to 80 million tonnes in 1992 from 37 million in 1980. However, the Japanese do not consider China to be as serious a competitor as South Korea. Steel exports from South Korea in 1991 totaled 7.7 million tonnes, compared with 4.6 million in 1981. This growth in exports reflects growth in South Korea's steel production, which rose from 10,753,000 tonnes in 1981 to 26,125,000 tonnes in 1991. Indeed, South Korea now ships considerable tonnage to Japan and competes with Japanese firms in their home market. In 1992 South Korea shipped 2,378,000 tonnes of steel products to Japan, while at the same time receiving 1,973,000 tonnes from Japan. Another nation considered to be a serious competitor by the Japanese is Taiwan, which exported a formidable 1,754,000 tonnes in 1990, providing competition for Japan in the export market.

Competition between developing and industrial countries is also manifested in the increase in exports from developing countries to industrialized countries. Those exports compete with the domestic production of the industrialized countries, as well as with exports from other industrialized countries.

It is interesting to note that the increase in exports from developing countries is associated principally with five nations, including Brazil, whose exports rose from 1.5 million tonnes in 1980 to 10.9 million tonnes in 1991, and South Korea, whose exports rose from 4.5 million tonnes in 1980 to 7.7 million tonnes in 1991. There was also a significant increase in exports from Taiwan, from 769,000 tonnes in 1980 to 1.8 million tonnes in 1990. Mexico's exports increased from a mere 67,000 tonnes in 1980 to 1.4 million tonnes in 1990. Meanwhile, Argentina witnessed a growth from 286,000 tonnes in 1980 to 2 million tonnes in 1990. These increases corresponded to a significant increase in steel production in three of the five countries enumerated. Brazil's production rose from 15.4 million tonnes in 1980 to 22.6 million tonnes in 1991, South Korea increased its production from 8.6 million tonnes in 1980 to 26 million tonnes in 1991, and Taiwan increased its output of crude steel from 3.4 million tonnes in 1980 to 11 million tonnes in 1991.

In 1974 exports from developing countries to the United States were relatively small. Mexico, for example, exported 121,000 tonnes, Brazil shipped 65,000 tonnes, and Argentina 166,000 tonnes. In 1980 exports from Mexico fell to 67,000 tonnes, but Brazil's exports increased to 458,000 tonnes. In 1991 exports from Mexico rose to 500,000 tonnes, those from Brazil to 1.5 million, and those from Argentina to 194,000 tonnes. Over the same period exports from South Korea to the United States increased from 863,000 tonnes to 1.4 million tonnes. Taiwan increased its exports to the United States from 95,000 tonnes in 1974 to 252,000 tonnes in 1987. These five countries are indicative of the growth of developing world exports, which totaled some 29 million tonnes in 1990 as compared with approximately 10 million tonnes in 1981. The increase in developing country steel exports to the United States has replaced much of the Japanese tonnage which dropped from a high point of 7.6 million tonnes in 1977 to 3.2 million in 1990.

Future Growth and Decline

The steel industry in the industrialized world is no longer a growth industry. Production in the individual countries, such as those in Western Europe, the United States, Canada, and Japan has been relatively stagnant for the past ten years. For example, in the EC output fluctuated between 123 million tonnes and 140 million tonnes during the 1980s; in 1992 output stood at 132 million tonnes. In the United States output reached a high of 109 million tons in 1981. Thereafter, it remained in the 80-million-ton range. In Japan, during the 1980s, production fluctuated from a high of 109 million tonnes in 1989 to a low of 97 million tonnes in 1983. Thus, although there were fluctuations, no appreciable growth took place. In the developing countries, however, production more than doubled between 1980 and 1992, rising from 102 million tonnes to 214 million tonnes.

In the early 1990s the High Commission for the European Community in Belgium decided that there was considerable overcapacity in the EC and proposed reducing steel production capacity by some 30 million tonnes over two or three years. If enacted, this cut would be the second major reduction in steel-making capacity in the EC. The first cut, of some 30 million tonnes, took place between 1980 and 1983.

The recent reduction figure was arrived at by calculating the rate of operations in the steel industry through 1991 and 1992. The capacity in existence in those years was judged to be 197.9 million tonnes, while reported production was 132 million tonnes in 1992. Based on a capacity of 197.0 million tonnes, the operating rate was 72 percent. The High Commission wanted to boost the operating rate to 85 percent. This could be done by reducing capacity by 30 million tonnes to 167 million tonnes; a production level of 140 million tonnes would be approximately 85 percent of capacity. Further, exports outside the EC, which were some 25 million tonnes, are declining because countries to which steel used to be exported have built up their own steel-making capacity and developing countries are increasing exports of steel to a number of areas throughout the world to which the EC also exports. Thus, it is calculated by some experts that in a matter of years, perhaps as few as seven or eight, EC exports outside the group itself will have dwindled to virtually nothing. Consequently, much existing EC capacity is not needed and should be eliminated. According to High Commission's judgment, an output of 160 million tonnes should be adequate to meet all EC needs.

The closure of these 30 million tonnes will result in social costs, including the loss of at least 70,000 jobs. The funds to meet these costs will come from several sources. One is the budget of the EC itself, into which the steel companies have been paying for years in the form of a levy on production. This is part of the contribution to the cost of workers leaving the company. The rest comes from member states whose contribution is equal to their contribution to the EC budget. These two sources are required for the costs of people who become unemployed. In addition, the industrial cost will be shouldered by companies that are remaining open; those that stay open will pay other companies for the capacity they close.

In Japan, capacity was reduced from 150 million tonnes in the late 1970s and early 1980s to approximately 125 million tonnes by the early 1990s. In 1987 the Japanese industry was considering an industry-wide 20-million-tonnes reduction in steel output. In 1988, however, after the Japanese government invested considerable money in the economy, steel production actually increased, rising to 110 million tonnes in 1991. It dropped back, however, to 98 million tonnes in 1992. Thus, with the decline in exports, as well as a decline in home consumption, there has been a significant reduction in capacity during the late 1980s. The EC, Japan, and the United States in total reduced capacity by about 100 million tonnes.

In the United States, with a loss of capacity of 45 million net tons, none of the integrated companies are planning any increase in steel production for the remainder of the present decade. There will be some minor increase in output as a consequence of the construction of three of four minimills for the production of flat products. In Japan, no increase has been planned by the integrated companies. In fact, some are trimming back to a minor extent. Thus, the total industrialized world will witness a decline in steelmaking capacity by the end of the century of perhaps 35 million to 40 million tonnes.

In contrast, the developing countries have significant expansion plans. The outstanding country in this respect is the People's Republic of China. Between 1980 and 1992 its crude steel production grew from 37 million tonnes to 80 million tonnes, and there is a plan to increase Chinese output to 100 million tonnes by the year 2000.

A Country-by-Country Review of the Steel Industry

A review of future steel plans for selected industrialized countries as well as those of developing countries will present a picture of the steel industry for the start of the twenty-first century.

Japan

Indicative of the decline in the Japanese steel industry are the figures for capital expenditures projected in 1993. Of the six major integrated steel-producing companies, five have reduced their capital expenditures for the fiscal year 1993. The one exception is Kawasaki Steel, which has increased its capital expenditures for that period. The total overall reduction has amounted to 24 percent from the previous fiscal year. Thus, for the first time in years, Japanese steel investments will decline significantly.

Nippon Steel plans to spend US$1.53 billion, down 15 percent. Much of this money will be used to complete projects that are currently under construction, including a new galvanizing line, a cold-rolling mill for stainless steel, and the rebuilding of a blast furnace. Further, this investment will also cover nonsteel activity.

NKK has reduced its capital expenditures to US$1.32 billion, down some 30 percent. Here again, the expenditures will be used to complete facilities already under construction, including a pulverized coal–injection system at the No. 4 blast furnace in Fukuyama, as well as a galvanizing line and other renovations to rolling mills. Again, the investment will also cover nonsteel items.

Kawasaki is the exception in the Japanese steel industry: it is increasing its capital investment to some $409 million per year for the years 1993 through 1995. Much of this money is intended for improvements at its Chiba works, including a new steel melting shop and a new continuous caster.

Sumitomo has reduced its capital spending to $1.18 billion,

a drop of approximately 30 percent, much of which will be spent on its pipe facilities at Wakayama.

Kobe Steel has reduced its capital expenditures to $955 million, a drop of some 43 percent. This investment will be directed to items that will save on costs and increase efficiency. They include a coil-coating line, a pulverized coal–injection facility at one of its blast furnaces, and the renovation of a hot-strip mill.

Nisshin, the smallest of the Japanese group, is reducing its capital expenditure to $264 million, a drop of some 41 percent. Much of its investment in the previous year as well as in the 1993 fiscal year is intended for a new blast furnace scheduled for completion by the end of the 1993 fiscal year.

The minimill segment of the Japanese steel industry, consisting of many small companies with a total capacity of some 30 million tonnes, will invest considerable capital. A number of these companies are owned either entirely or in part by the major integrated companies. There are two, independents, Yamato Steel, which is in the business of producing structural sections, and Tokyo Steel, which produces structural sections, but is also involved in the production of flat-rolled products, particularly hot-rolled bands.

Tokyo Steel entered the flat-rolled segment within the last two years; in 1992 it produced some 700,000 tonnes. The mill is located at its Okayama plant, about 100 miles east of Hiroshima. In 1993 production was between 1 and 1.2 million tonnes; Tokyo Steel hopes to increase this output in 1994 to 1.5 million tonnes, the ultimate capacity of the plant. At the same location, the company produces structural sections. This plant is to be closed down, however, and moved to another location, the Utsunomita works, where a plant is under construction that will produce 800,000 tonnes of structural sections. The basic reason for the closure is the lack of scrap in the Okayoma area, particularly as Tokyo hopes to increase its production of light, flat-rolled products, and thus requires more scrap. The new structural mill, which is in fact a replacement facility, will be in operation at the end of 1995 and will involve an investment of some $400 million. The company has also announced construction plans for a new flat-rolled plant with about 800,000 to 1 million tonnes of capacity to be located at Yokkaichi near Nagoya. This project is now under study. A decision has not yet been made as to whether a thin-slab caster will be installed. The plant is scheduled to go into operation in 1996 at an estimated cost of approximately $400 million. Thus, capacity for flat-rolled products will be increased, whereas capacity for the production of structural sections will not be increased, since the new plant at the Utsunomita works is a replacement for that at Okayama.

The total industry capital expenditures projected for the fiscal year 1993 are $6.6 billion. Although this amount represents a significant reduction from the previous year, it is in keeping with the rate of investment made by the Japanese steel industry throughout the 1980s. During that ten-year period the Japanese steel industry invested $34 billion, some of which was assigned to the various other activities in which the steel companies were engaged.

Japan's steel industry has a number of overseas investments, many of which were made in the steel industry in the United States. Japan's steel industry has invested $2 billion in U.S. projects. Japan has also entered into a number of joint ventures with steel companies in Southeast Asia. Nippon Steel has invested in Thai Siam Tinplate, NKK has invested in Thai Coated Steel for galvanized production, and Kobe has invested in Thai Wire. In Indonesia, Nippon and Mitsui are combining to invest in a galvanized sheet operation, as is NKK and Marubeni. Nippon is engaged in a project with ISPAT to build a sheet mill in India; this facility is scheduled to have a 2-million-tonne hot-strip mill, based on direct-reduced iron (DRI) and electric-furnace production that will be coupled to a thin-slab caster. Sumitomo has invested in a pipe plant in Thailand with Thai Steel Pipe Company. The Thai company was established in 1963; 50 percent of its capital is held by Sumitomo, 25 percent by Nomura Trading Company, and 12½ percent each by Mitsui and Siam Steel Pipe.

NKK, through its manufacturing arm, has received five orders for DC electric furnaces from various places throughout the world. One will go to Bethlehem Steel in the United States, another to Taiwan's Wei Chi Steel Industries, two furnaces will go to Han Bo in South Korea, and one to Japan's Toa Steel Company, a 150-tonne twin furnace.

The Japanese steel industry has become highly diversified. All the major companies are involved in an aluminum operation, among other things. In the future, Japan's steel capacity will remain relatively stable, with emphasis on quality and costs as well as the export of high-value steel products. One example of this emphasis is the group formed by the Science and Technology Agency of the Ministry of International Trade and Industry (MITI). This group, which encompasses all six major steel companies, is expected to participate in a project to create the next generation of coke ovens through the Japan Iron and Steel Federation. The entire project will involve an investment in excess of $90 million. According to a government official, "There is a need to develop next generation coking ovens because the old ovens will have to be replaced but only by environmentally friendly ones. This next generation of coke ovens will have two innovations; it will be able to use steam coal, and it will emit very little nitro oxide and no carbon dioxide, since it will employ a closed system."[2]

In contrast to the situation in the 1970s and early 1980s, Japan will import a significant tonnage of steel, somewhere in the area of 7–10 million tonnes per year, which will come principally from developing countries.

United States

In the decade of the 1980s the steel industry in the United States invested $23 billion in plants and equipment. A great deal of modernization was achieved, particularly through the installation of continuous casters so that the percentage of steel cast rose from 20 percent in 1980 to 80 percent in 1992.

During the present decade capital expenditures will be less than they were in the 1980s, although the total for 1990 through 1992 was some $8.3 billion. Expenditures for the middle of the decade will be on a somewhat smaller scale since most of the major modernization programs have already been completed. They will pick up again toward the decade's close.

Production in 1992 was 83.2 million metric tonnes. In 1993 output rose to 85 million metric tonnes, which was well within the industry's capacity. The rate of operating capacity for the year was 87 percent.

There are no plans to increase capacity among the integrated producers in the United States, since that which is currently in operation is adequate to take care of demand for most of the rest of the decade. The capacity of the integrated producers may decline to a slight extent between now and the year 2000. However, this decline will be compensated by an increase in capacity among the minimills of some 5 million to 6 million tons. Several minimill installations using thin-slab casters have been planned; these will add a relatively small amount to the industry's capacity. Two minimills are operating thin-slab casters at the present time. Additional capacity will come through the expansion of these existing mills as well as through the installation of several new ones.

On a company-by-company basis, the planned activity in terms of capital spending reveals concern about improving quality and reducing costs rather than increasing steelmaking capacity. A review of the companies' recent installations and future plans bears this out. The steel industry in the United States is divided into two categories, integrated companies and minimills.

Integrated Companies.

United States Steel. United States Steel is trying to keep its capital expenditures for the next few years in line with its depreciation, which is $250–$300 million, depending on the rate of operations. Much was done in the 1980s to modernize plant and equipment. Capital expenditures made from 1988 through 1992 amounted to $2 billion. Major projects included the installation of continuous casters, such as the unit installed in the Pittsburgh district at a cost of $250 million, as well as two units installed at the Gary, Indiana, plant. Further, the Gary No. 13 blast furnace, the largest in the corporation, was relined at a cost of $100 million, and coal-injection systems were installed at four of the Gary blast furnaces at a cost in excess of $75 million. Major adjustments to the Gary hot-strip mill cost $100 million. Total expenditures at Gary from 1989 through 1992 amounted to $780 million.

In terms of investment in its joint ventures, United States Steel invested $200 million at the Lorain, Ohio, plant, which it jointly owns with Kobe Steel of Japan. The $200 million was United States Steel's share of plant modernization costs. The corporation also invested $100 million in a joint venture with Kobe Steel to build a galvanizing line located at Leipsic, Ohio. In the late 1980s a joint venture with Pohang Iron and Steel Company of Korea at Pittsburg, California, required a total investment of some $500 million, of which United States Steel supplied half.

One joint venture that is contemplated in conjunction with Worthington Corporation is the construction of a thin-slab caster hot-strip mill complex with 2 million tons of capacity at a cost in excess of $400 million. Costs will be borne equally by United States Steel and Worthington. This mill will increase the corporation's current capacity. However, if built, the new mill will be a joint venture, so that only 50 percent of output, or 1 million tons, will be added to United States Steel's steelmaking potential.

United States Steel feels that its investments have modernized the company significantly, so that for the next two or three years it can be content with expenditures that total depreciation costs. Recognizing that modernization is a continuing operation, United States Steel will likely resume heavy capital investment after 1995.

Bethlehem Steel. Among the integrated companies, Bethlehem Steel is rated No. 2 in size and has plans for investment in plant and equipment to be undertaken in the remainder of the 1990s. One of these was the restructuring of its large structural operation at Bethlehem, Pennsylvania. Bethlehem had committed $100 million principally to install an electric furnace, a variable-beam caster as well as to upgrade the rolling mill and increase process control. Very recently this plan has been abandoned, since Bethlehem is exiting the production of large wide-flange beams over 27 inches. The steelmaking facilities at its Bethlehem plant will ultimately be closed down and blooms for the production of medium-sized and small structurals will be obtained from the rejuvenated plant at Steelton, a subsidiary now known as Pennsylvania Steel Technologies, Inc. The phase out of large beams at Bethlehem will be completed in 1996.

At the Steelton location, some $80 million has been invested to upgrade the electric furnaces by installing a DC furnace to be purchased from NKK of Japan. In addition to the new furnace, the heat treating of rails will be upgraded to make them a world-class product.

Another investment is the rebuilding of a coke-oven at Burns Harbor and the installation of coal-injection systems at the two blast furnaces located there. The cost of the latter was $135 million. Annual capital expenditures for 1993 were $353 million and should be approximately the same or somewhat higher in 1994. Improvements are designed to reduce costs and upgrade quality without any addition to production capacity.

LTV Steel. LTV is the third largest integrated steel producer in the U.S. with plants in Cleveland, Ohio and Indiana Harbor, Indiana. The company has just completed a major project at its Cleveland plant involving a continuous caster as well as direct steel rolling. The work was completed over a two-year span at a cost of $312 million.

Recently, the company has expressed a very definite interest in the Corex process. It is contemplating building a new type of facility, capable of producing 1 million tons, or three times the output of the Corex facility currently operating at ISCOR in South Africa. The engineering and development phases of the project are currently underway but a firm decision to install it has not yet been made. Very serious consideration is being given to the Corex unit by LTV and its two partners, namely, Air Products and Cleveland Electric Company. Total projected cost is in the area of $800 million, but the Department of Energy is making a grant of $150 million of the cost. This facility will act as a partial replacement for blast furnace capacity in the Cleveland district.

LTV's investments during the coming years, in addition to the possibility of buying a Corex unit, will be made to improve quality and reduce costs.

Armco Inc. Armco Inc. has recently announced a radical change in its corporate structure. The joint venture with Kawasaki Steel of Japan that consists of two plants located at Middletown, Ohio, and Ashland, Kentucky, is very much involved. These two plants will constitute an independent company named AK Steel. Kawasaki will retain some 21 percent ownership, while the parent company, Armco, will retain less than 1 percent and the AK Steel pension fund will own 10 to 11 percent. The income from the sale of stock will be used for a number of purposes among which is paying off debts. Armco Inc. will remain in the specialty steel business with its principal plant at Butler, Pennsylvania. It will also operate a smaller plant, Empire Steel, at Mansfield, Ohio where it has invested $100 million for the installation of a thin-slab caster that will replace the ingot process at the plant.

Inland Steel. Inland has invested considerable money in the last few years. Much of it was spent on a joint venture with Nippon Steel which included installing a cold-reduction mill and two galvanizing lines at New Carlisle, Indiana. The total cost of the project was $1.1 billion, with Inland assuming 60 percent of the cost of the cold-reduction mill and 50 percent of the cost of the galvanizing lines.

Inland also invested $200 million in its Indiana Harbor plant, much of which was used to upgrade its hot-strip mill to produce quality sheets to feed the new cold-reduction mill. Now that these projects have been completed, Inland is in the process of making them operate at their full potential. As a consequence, the company has no major projects planned for the immediate future, but does intend to spend millions of dollars on a group of relatively small items.

National Steel. National has been involved in a joint venture with NKK of Japan since 1984. Currently, NKK owns 76 percent of National. The company has recently completed the construction of a 900,000-ton coke-oven battery at a cost in excess of $300 million. Presently, it is involved in the construction of a pickle line at its Great Lakes division and also a joint venture with Bethlehem Steel on a galvanizing line in Mississippi.

Wheeling-Pittsburgh. Wheeling-Pittsburgh has plans to improve its blast furnace operation by replacing the bosh of one furnace and upgrading the other furnaces, so that ultimately the company will be able to produce its iron from two furnaces rather than three. These renovations will be achieved at a cost of $70 million.

Weirton Steel. Weirton, one of the smaller integrated companies, spent $500 million over a period of three years from 1989 to 1992; $200 million of this money was invested in a complete rebuilding of the hot-strip mill and $70 million was used to upgrade the continuous caster.

The company studied the possibility of a thin-slab caster as well as a new conventional unit but decided the investment to upgrade the existing facility was considerably less than either of the other two alternatives. Currently, Weirton is spending its capital on relatively small projects.

Minimills. The minimill sector of the U.S. steel industry is a special part of the whole. It consists of some thirty companies, operating some fifty plants throughout the country. There are several relatively large companies in this sector of the industry.

Nucor. Perhaps the most outstanding company among the minimills is Nucor which has six plants scattered throughout the United States, two of which produce light, flat-rolled products with the use of thin-slab casters. One is located at Crawfordsville, Indiana, and the other at Hickman, Arkansas. Each plant is currently capable of producing approximately 1 million tons. However, Nucor is installing an additional thin-slab caster at each facility; these additions will double output at both locations. This will be accomplished with a relatively small investment of some $40 million and a 10 percent increase in the work force. Thus, between the two plants, Nucor will boost its capacity to produce sheets to about 4 million tons.

Nucor is also investing $60 million in an iron-carbide production facility on the island of Trinidad. This material will be used to supplement the scrap charge at its two plants in order to dilute impurities in the scrap to produce a better grade of steel. This plant will be the first production unit for the manufacture of iron carbide.

Nucor also has a joint venture with Yamato of Japan for the production of structural steel which is being expanded.

Birmingham Steel. Birmingham, one of the larger minimill complexes, has a total of six plants in the United States, all producing conventional minimill products. The company places particular emphasis on rebar and mine-roof bolts. It is improving a number of its plants, particularly one in Seattle where capacity will be raised by 50 percent. This will be achieved by replacing two AC electric furnaces with one DC furnace having a 150-ton capacity. An investment of roughly $30 million will provide metal for its recently installed rolling equipment.

Birmingham acquired American Steel and Wire Corporation, which has a plant at Cuyahoga Heights, near Cleveland, Ohio. This acquisition will put Birmingham into the rod business. American Steel and Wire was formerly part of United States Steel and depends on purchased billets since it has no steelmaking equipment.

North Star. North Star is another minimill with six plants. Currently, it plans to more than double capacity at its Saint Paul, Minnesota, plant, increasing output from 300,000 tons to 650,000 tons by mid-1995. The investment required is estimated at $40 million. North Star will replace two electric-arc furnaces with a single DC furnace and a ladle furnace, changes that will permit the plant to improve the quality of its steel production and bring total output of its plants to 2.5 million tons.

Recently, North Star announced that it will build a new minimill with 500,000 tons of capacity at a cost of $100 million to produce standard minimill products including concrete reinforcing bar, small structurals, and wire rods. The plant will be located in either Arizona or Nevada to serve the West Coast market where other minimills have closed down, but where demand for minimill products continues to grow.

The company is engaged in a series of talks with Broken Hill Proprietary (BHP) of Australia to build a joint-venture, thin-slab-sheet plant somewhere in the western part of the United States. As yet no final decision has been made on this project.

North Star is a subsidiary of Cargill, which is cash-rich, and consequently has funds available to expand and develop its facilities.

Oregon Steel. This company has its principal facility near Portland, Oregon, where it produces products to serve the West Coast market. The company produces plates and has recently acquired CF&I, located in Pueblo, Colorado. CF&I was in Chapter 11 bankruptcy when it was purchased. Oregon intends to invest approximately $150 million to install a rod mill and upgrade the facilities to improve rail production at CF&I.

Oregon has recently entered into a joint venture with Nucor to build a 1-million-ton plant based on an electric furnace with direct-reduced iron (DRI) as part of the charge. The plant will have a thin-slab caster and a rolling mill. Currently, the partners are searching for a site on the West Coast in northern California, Washington, or Oregon. The mill will produce hot-rolled sheets from a strip mill with six stands 60-inches wide. These will serve the West Coast market which presently has an adequate capacity in place to supply its needs. It faces competition from California Steel at Fontana, as well as from USS/POSCO located in Pittsburg, California, which produces cold-rolled sheets, tinplate, and galvanized sheets from hot-rolled bands that are shipped to the plant from both South Korea and United States Steel mills in the United States. The new Oregon Steel/Nucor mill will have hot-rolled as well as cold-rolled sheets available for sale. The current arrangement is 60 percent ownership by Nucor and 40 percent by Oregon Steel.

Northwestern Steel & Wire. Northwestern has two plants, one in Sterling, Illinois, and the other in Houston, Texas. The latter was formerly owned by Armco Inc. For years the company has produced structural sections from electric-furnace steel but now it plans to diversify into slab production at its Sterling plant to take advantage of the growing slab needs of the U.S. integrated steelmakers. A slab caster will be installed with a capacity of 1 million tons. The company is also planning to increase its structural capacity at Houston by 750,000 tons.

California Steel. Its plant at Fontana, California, was formerly Kaiser Steel and is now owned on a 50–50 basis by Kawasaki Steel of Japan and CVRD, a Brazilian ore company. It has been operating on purchased slabs, principally from Brazil, although it does use some domestic sources.

The company produces hot- and cold-rolled sheets, galvanized steel, and tinplate. It has recently received approval from its owners to conduct a feasibility study looking to install a melt shop with a DC furnace along with a ladle furnace and a continuous caster to produce slabs. Total investment would be $150–$170 million. This would provide the company with its own steel and reduce the need to purchase outside slabs. It will place the company in the category of a steel producer rather than a rolling operation.

The addition of the melt shop will increase the melting capacity of the U.S. steel industry by at least 1 million tons, although it will not increase the output of California Steel, since it is substituting slabs made on the premises for those that are purchased.

California has recently sold its BOF steel shop and its continuous caster to the Chinese. These units have not been operated for a number of years.

Beta Steel. A recent addition to the U.S. steel industry is Beta Steel, which installed a hot-strip mill with some 800,000 tons of capacity in northern Indiana in 1991. This mill was transported from Alpha's steel plant in England and installed in the United States. Beta Steel depends on purchased slabs since it has no steelmaking capacity. In September 1993 it announced a planned expansion to include the installation of two electric furnaces and a second hot-strip mill. The electric furnaces will have a capacity of some 800,000 tons and the new hot-strip mill will bring the rolling-mill capacity up to 1.5 million tons. This means that Beta Steel will still have to depend on at least 500,000 tons of purchased slabs to fill its operating capacity.

Ipsco Inc. Ipsco, a plate mill based in western Canada, has announced plans to build a minimill for the production of plates and sheets in the Midwestern United States. The site has not yet been chosen, although consideration is being given to possible locations in Kentucky. The plant will consist of a DC electric furnace, a continuous slab-casting mill, and a steckle rolling mill. Plate will constitute 75 percent of the output made from six-inch slabs. The capacity of the mill will be 1 million tons, at a cost of some $360 million. Three-fourths of the output will be in plate and the remaining 25 percent in hot-rolled sheets.

It is evident from the foregoing analysis that any significant increase in steel production in the United States will be made by the minimill segment of the industry. In 1992, it produced 34 million net tons, or 37 percent, of a total U.S. steel output of 93 million net tons, while the integrated segment produced 58 million net tons, or 63 percent of the total. The percentage of minimill production will most probably be between 42 and 45 percent by the year 2000, judging from the projected increases in steel which they plan to make as well as the fact that a few million tons of integrated capacity could be withdrawn.

The European Community

As previously indicated, the High Commission of the European Community in Brussels is attempting to reduce raw-steel capacity in the EC by some 30 million tonnes. It is expected that each of the major countries will make a contribution to this reduction. The plans and position of some senior members of the EC indicate what will be done in this respect.

United Kingdom. The principal steel company in the United Kingdom is British Steel, which was founded in 1967 by the nationalization of more than 70 percent of the British steel industry. At that time, it had a capacity to produce 28 million tonnes. Fourteen companies and twenty-two plants were involved in the nationalization project. During the 1970s and early 1980s capacity was reduced to the current level of 14–15 million tonnes. In 1988–89 British Steel was privatized through the sale of shares worth £2.8 billion.

During the last decade the corporation invested large sums in capital equipment. In several of the last few years capital investment was in excess of £300 million. In 1989 £307 million was invested, embracing a number of facilities. At the Trostre plant a continuous-annealing line was installed at a cost of £47 million. At Llanwern, a continuous-casting facility was installed at a cost of £47 million. Between 1990 and 1992 an electrolytic galvanizing line was installed at Shotten, a pickling line was installed at Port Talbot for £36 million, a hot-dipped galvanizing line was installed at Llanwern for £59 million, a universal beam mill at Teesside was modernized for £69 million, and a second continuous-caster was added at Port Talbot for £70 million. These investments modernized the corporation considerably. As a consequence, no major investment in capital equipment is anticipated for the near future. The corporation has a series of small projects, none of which is particularly impressive.

British Steel in completing these various projects will spend less than £200 million a year during the next few years. There are no plans to invest significant amounts of capital in large projects. A new plate mill intended to replace two existing plate mills, estimated to cost £400 million, had been considered during the past few years, but has now been put on hold indefinitely.

Along with all the other steel companies in the EC, British Steel was requested to consider a reduction in capacity. However, since the corporation had reduced its capacity by 50 percent during its existence, a further reduction, if any, will be relatively small.

There are several significant minimills in the United Kingdom, including United Engineering Steels (UES), with a capacity of 2 million tonnes; Alpha Steel, with a capacity of 1.5 million tonnes; Sheerness, which is owned by CoSteel of Canada, with approximately 1 million tonnes of capacity dedicated to the production of minimill products such as reinforcing bars and light structurals; and Allied Steel and Wire, a minimill located in Cardiff with a capacity of 1 million tonnes dedicated to the production of wire rods, reinforcing bars, light angles, channels, and narrow flat sections. There is little indication that any of these minimills will enter the production of flat-rolled products. Alpha Steel produced fairly large tonnages of flat-rolled products several years ago. However, since then it has sold its slab caster to British Steel and removed its strip mill to northern Indiana in the United States, where a new company, Beta Steel, has been established. Sheerness Steel has no current intention of moving into the flat-rolled steel business.

Germany. Germany has been the leading steel producer in the EC since 1950 when the union was formed. It reached a high peak of production in 1974 with 53 million tonnes of raw steel. Since 1991, steel statistics concerning Germany have included the output of what was formerly East Germany. In that year, raw steel production reached 42.2 million tonnes. In the last year for which statistics were given for West Germany alone, output stood at 38.4 million tonnes. In 1992 production for the reunited Germany stood at 39.8 million tonnes.

Currently, Germany has five integrated steel companies and some fourteen plants that are considered minimills. The largest integrated company in Germany is Thyssen Steel, which has a production capacity of approximately 10 million tonnes of raw steel. At one time it had as much as 20-million-tonnes of capacity. The company has had a sizeable capital investment program during the past few years. In 1992 capital expenditures amounted to 1.8 billion marks. In 1993 the figure fell to 1.1 billion marks. For 1994 an investment of 1 billion marks is projected. The most significant facilities installed during this period were a 10,000-tonne-a-day blast furnace, at a cost of 780 million marks, and a galvanizing line; still under construction are a coating line and a Zendzimir mill. For 1995, capital expenditures will be virtually equivalent to depreciation charges.

Thyssen in conjunction with Usinor has been working on a thin-slab process that will cast a slab or possibly a sheet of one-half-inch thickness. It will require just a one-stand rolling mill to reduce the item to sheet thickness, and it is estimated that by the year 2000 25 percent of the sheets could well be produced from thin-slab casters with one rolling stand.

Thyssen laid off some 6,500 people in 1993 and will reduce its work force by more than 6,000 in 1994. People at age fifty-four are encouraged to retire with a separation figure of 40,000 to 60,000 marks. They will receive 90 percent of their net income until age 60, after which they will receive pensions.

The second largest company in Germany was formed as the result of a merger between Krupp and Hoesch and now has approximately 8–9 million tonnes of raw steel capacity. In the consolidation of facilities, two plants have been closed, one at Rheinhausen and the other at Oranienburg. In the past few years both companies have invested significant sums of capital to upgrade hot-strip mills and cold-reduction mills. As a consequence of these improvements, the amount of capital to be expended in the years immediately ahead will be considerably reduced. In fact, it probably will not amount to the full depreciation charges for the next two to three years.

As part of the modernization program, Krupp commissioned a 500,000-tonne hot-dipped galvanizing line at Bochum in late June 1992. The investment amounted to 300 million marks and was one of the most significant that Krupp has made in the last few years. Also late in 1992, Krupp started up a new cold-rolling mill for stainless and heat-resistant steel at Dillenburg. The mill can produce coils of up to 30 tonnes, to 1315mm wide, to 0.15mm thick.

Krupp/Hoesch has laid off 13,000 people in 1993 and will lay off many in 1994. The company is looking to Eastern Europe as a major market for its steel in the next five to six years.

Klockner, another integrated steel company in Germany, has been in financial trouble in recent years and has declared bankruptcy. The company has closed down several of its facilities in Bremen and has sold another part of its facilities to Jurgen Grossman. The plant acquired by Grossman, Klockner Edelstahl, will replace its existing blast furnace and oxygen-converter shop with an electric-arc furnace. This will cut raw steel capacity from 900,000 tonnes to 600,000 tonnes and reduce the work force by 23 percent. The rolling mill is in excellent condition Grossman says, "We have one of the best rolling mills in Europe for bar steels so that we have a competitive steel-making facility as well. Where we are it cannot be done with a blast furnace and converter. There is a lot of scrap in our area and at the moment it is mainly exported."[3]

There are two problem areas in the German steel industry in regard to reduction of capacity. One is the Klockner Works at Bremen. A number of German steel industrialists believe that the steelmaking segment of this plant and its hot-strip mill should be closed, with operations henceforth confined to finishing facilities. Klockner's debt is approximately 175 million marks, about $110 million. A significant percentage of this debt will be written off if Klockner makes a binding commitment to reduce its capacity. The company offered a capacity reduction of 20 percent. To solve the problem, Thyssen and Krupp/Hoesch have indicated that they would buy the rolling facilities and close the iron and steelmaking segments and the hot-strip mill. A counteroffer was made by the city of Bremen, which wanted to protect 2,600 jobs that would be lost if much of the plant were to be closed. The proposition offered by the city has been accepted. The city will sell selected municipal assets in order to finance the operation. Thus, the steel capacity at Klockner will remain intact for at least a few years. This transaction is under review by the High Commission in Brussels.

The other company that has a capacity problem is EKO Steel in the former East Germany. This mill, which has operated for a number of years, is located near the Polish border. The plant has ironmaking and steelmaking capacity through the use of a blast furnace and a basic-oxygen shop. However, it does not have a hot-strip mill, and consequently its slabs had to be sent out to be rolled by other mills and then returned for cold reduction at EKO. The fate of the mill was very much in question, since German steel industry representatives felt that it is needlessly contributing to overcapacity in the country. There are, however, steel people who wanted to see EKO turned into a sizeable electric-furnace operation. Some talked about installing a thin-slab caster and a hot-strip mill. The Italians in the person of Riva as well as some Germans are interested in such an operation, while Thyssen and Krupp/Hoesch are interested in acquiring the finishing facilities and shutting down the basic steel operation. Thyssen and Krupp/Hoesch would keep the cold-rolling and other finishing facilities intact; they have offered to guarantee finding jobs for the thousand people who would be laid off as a result of the closure of the steelmaking facilities.

A proposition offered by Riva, an Italian steel producer, would maintain all of the facilities at EKO and add a hot-strip mill. Riva would have 60 percent of the ownership and the state would have 40 percent. This would be the third venture of Riva in Germany. The other two that have been purchased recently are bar mills, one at Brandenberg and one at Henningsdorfer, each with 1 million tonne capacity. EKO will have a capacity to produce 2 million tonnes of sheets; however, Riva has plans to hold production to 900,000 tonnes a year for five years. The state will contribute funds for the construction of the hot strip mill and for the modernization of the cold reduction mill. The hot strip mill will most likely come from Iran and the cold mill modernization will be expensive.

In terms of minimill competition with integrated mills, it consists in the production of bars and rods. This will most probably fade out as integrated mills reduce their production of these items. In terms of competition in flat-rolled products between minimills and integrated mills, it is not likely that this will take place in the near future. This is particularly true since the integrated mills have a cost structure that is equivalent to any projected minimill operating costs. Further, there is overcapacity at the present time, which means that very little money will be available for new capacity to produce sheets.

France. The steel industry of France is dominated by state owned Usinor Sacilor Steel Company. In 1991 and 1992 this company was the second largest steel producer in the world, surpassed only by Nippon Steel of Japan. Usinor had an output in excess of

21.1 million tonnes in 1992, while Nippon registered 25.4 million tonnes of crude steel. Interestingly enough, because of Usinor's holdings in other countries, the company's output of 21.1 million tonnes exceeded the total output of France, which was 18 million tonnes. The company had a significant operation in Germany at Saarstahl which it subsequently relinquished.

In the past decade Usinor spent several billion dollars on plant and equipment. Toward the end of that period, two galvanizing lines, one coating line, and a 700,000-tonne electric-arc furnace were installed, along with vacuum-degassing. In the current decade Usinor plans to install an additional electric furnace that will take the place of a blast furnace and a basic-oxygen converter and reduce one of its plant's capacity from 2.2 million tonnes to 1.3 million tonnes. This is part of Usinor's contribution to the EC reduction in steelmaking capacity. Having invested very heavily in the 1980s, Usinor will not invest its depreciation in 1993, but will see to it that the facilities throughout the company are maintained in excellent condition in regard to the attainment of low costs and high quality.

Usinor has made several agreements with Arbed regarding long products. Usinor moved out of the structural business, leaving it to Arbed, and Arbed moved out of the rod and rail business, leaving it to Usinor.

There has been some discussion concerning the privatization of Usinor, but this does not seem to be imminent.

Luxembourg. Arbed, the Luxemborg steel company, was the sixth largest producer of crude steel in the EC in 1992, with an output of 7.1 million tonnes. It is also one of the largest producers of structural steel in the EC.

During 1993, in order to face the crisis of steel overproduction in the EC, Arbed devised a plan to update its structural facilities that are located at three different plants, namely, Differdange, Esch-Schifflange, and Esch-Belval. These plants produced structural sections from steel produced via a blast furnace and basic-oxygen converters at Esch-Belval. Hot metal was transported to the other two plants where it was converted into steel by the basic-oxygen method. Arbed's plan involves an investment of 12.5 billion Luxembourg francs to replace the BOF units at Differdange and Esch-Schifflange. The new Esch-Schifflange furnace was completed in December 1993 and commissioned at that time. It is an AC electric unit with a 120-tonne heat capacity.

The second step in this modernization process involves the installation of a 155-tonne DC furnace at Differdange. This is currently under construction and should be in operation by mid-1994. A continuous caster that will produce near net-shape sections will also be installed. Further, the structural mill itself will be improved. Under study is the possible construction of an electric furnace at Esch-Belval; at which point, the two blast furnaces will be completely shut down.

In March 1992 Arbed acquired the Stahlwerk Thurigen plant in eastern Germany. The plant operated a blast furnace and a basic-oxygen converter. Arbed plans to replace these units with an electric furnace with a 120-tonne capacity as well as a ladle furnace, and a continuous beam, blank, and bloom caster. The investment required for these operations, which include the modernization of the rolling mill, will be some 300 million marks. The rolling mill has a capacity of almost 700,000 tonnes per year. However, it has been producing at a little more than half that rate, namely, 400,000 tonnes. With modernization and improvements, it will increase its production to some 500,000 tonnes.

In addition to updating the structural phase of Arbed's production, an improvement will be made to modernize its rod mill, which is now operated as a joint venture with Usinor/Sacilor and is located at Esch-Schifflange.

Arbed is reducing its labor force from 8,700 people to 6,700 people.

Italy. Italy with a production in 1992 of 24.9 million tonnes is one of the few countries in the industrialized world that has maintained its record 1974 output. In that year, it produced a then-record 23.8 million tonnes. Further, its electric-furnace steelmaking segment accounts for 59 percent of its total production, with oxygen contributing 41 percent. In 1993, the country produced a record raw steel tonnage of 25.9 million tonnes. This is remarkable when one considers that the steel industry in Italy was under a good deal of pressure during that time to reduce its steel capacity by more than 3 million tonnes.

The principal and only producer of basic-oxygen steel was ILVA, which has been dissolved. The dissolution of ILVA resulted in two companies, one, Ilva Laminata Piani, which will produce and market carbon flat-rolled products, and the other, Acciai Speciali Terni, which will take over and produce and market special flat products. Both companies are the subjects of privatization and several groups have expressed interest in acquiring each of the two companies. Ilva Laminata will operate Taranto as well as a number of other plants, while Acciai Speciali has taken over Terni as well as Torinox. The privatization will take place in the early spring of 1994.

The Riva interests have acquired 60 percent of EKO Steel in Germany with the obligation to install a hot-strip mill, that need not be new and could possibly be from Iran.

Turkey. Turkey has had a most significant increase in its steel industry during the past 15 years. In 1979, production was 2.4 million tonnes. By 1983, it had risen to 3.8 million, a relatively modest increase. However, by 1992, output surpassed 10 million tonnes. In 1993, it continued to increase its steel output to 11.4 million tonnes. The country has also been active in the export market. From virtually nothing in 1979, when it exported 6,000 tonnes, it increased its exports to over 4 million tonnes in 1991. The principal market for Turkish exports has been the Far East which received some 75 percent of the total in 1991.

In 1992, of the raw steel production of 10.3 million tonnes, 60 percent or roughly 6 million tonnes was made in the electric furnace, 34 percent or 3.4 million tonnes in the basic oxygen converter, and a relatively small 6 percent in the open hearth. In terms of continuous casting, in 1992 86.9 percent of the raw steel poured was continuously cast.

Turkey was considered a developing country in terms of steel output in the early 1980s. It has now reached the status of a substantial producer and exporter. In terms of the future, the principal integrated company, Eregli, is currently government-owned but will be privatized in the next year or at the most two. The growth in the past decade has been in the electric-furnace sector where a number of companies have been brought into being and others expanded.

Russia & Ukraine. The recent dissolution of the USSR has high-lighted some developments in its steel industry. The last year for which statistics for the Soviet Union are available is 1992, when the tonnage was estimated at 111,200,000 tonnes. This was a considerable drop from the previous year, 1991, when 132,839,000 tonnes were registered. In turn, this was a sharp decline from the high point of 163,037,000 in 1988. Recent statistics have been reported independently for Russia and the Ukraine as well as the other previous Soviet republics. For 1993, Russian production was 58,236,000 tonnes while that of the Ukraine was 30,537,000 tonnes. Kazakhstan recorded 4,279,000 tonnes and Belarus 766,000 tonnes, while Uzbeki-stan recorded 573,000 tonnes for a total of 94,391,000 tonnes. Much of this production came from open hearth furnaces.

In 1992, crude steel output for Russia was 67 million tonnes of which 34.5 percent was from the basic oxygen process, 15.4 percent from the electric-arc furnace, and 50.1 percent from the open hearth. Of the Ukrainian production of 41.7 million tonnes in 1992, 52.6 percent was made in the open hearth, 39.8 percent in the basic-oxygen converter, and 7.6 percent in the electric-arc furnace. In terms of continuous casting, in 1992, 27.9 percent of Russian steel was continuously cast and only 7.5 percent of Ukrainian steel. As a consequence, much modernization is

needed in both the Russian and Ukrainian steel industry to replace the open hearth and install more continuous casting. Some
plans are underway, but much will have to be done if these two
countries are to produce steel that will be generally competitive
in the world market.

Australia

In 1992 Australia produced 6,850,000 tonnes of raw steel. This
output was representative of production for the decade of the
1980s, which averaged about 6.4 million tonnes annually. Thus,
the amount of growth was minimal. Imports for the decade of
the 1980s averaged approximately 750,000 tonnes, while exports averaged 1 million tonnes, increasing to 2 million tonnes
in 1991.

The principal steel producer in Australia is Broken Hill Proprietary (BHP), which accounts for better than 95 percent of
steel output. During the coming years BHP plans to build a new
blast furnace at its Port Kembla plant that will replace the production of two blast furnaces currently operating, which will be
destroyed. The capacity of the new blast furnace will be 7,000
tonnes per day. The cost of the furnace will be in the area of
Aus.$400 million. It is scheduled to go into operation in early
1996. Some additional pig iron will be produced over and above
that which the two current furnaces produce, so that the plant's
actual capacity will be increased from 4 million tonnes to 4.3
million tonnes, or by approximately 7 percent. At the end of
1992 work has begun on upgrading a BHP blast furnace at
BHP's Whyalla works.

BHP recently commissioned a minimill in the Sydney area. It
was built at a cost of Aus.$300 million and will produce
250,000 tonnes of billets for BHP's rod and bar mills. It will
make 200,000 tonnes of BHP's Newcastle steel works' capacity
available for the production of special-quality bars. The second
stage of this minimill involves building facilities to produce rods
and bars and should be available in 1994.

Within the next few years BHP plans to build a number of

minimills, some of which may involve thin-slab casting technology. These will be located in countries outside Australia on the Pacific Rim. Possible locations include Vietnam, Sri Lanka, and China. These proposed installations are being justified on the basis of potential growth in steel demand in southeastern Asia.

In terms of finished product, BHP is constructing a coil-coating line at its Brisbane plant. Production will be approximately 45,000 tonnes of colored steel per year. The facility will be installed at a cost of Aus.$30 million.

BHP, in a joint venture with several east Asian partners, is also planning to build a 100,000-tonne-per-year aluminum-coating plant and a 50,000-tonne-a-year paint line in Java. The plant will be built next to the Krakatau steel mill for a total investment of Aus.$75 million. BHP will provide either slabs or hot-rolled coils to Krakatau for conversion into cold-rolled coils, which will then be used to feed the new line.

Recently a study has been made of the possibility of building a steel plant in western Australia for the production of 1.8 million tonnes of raw steel a year. The plant is being studied by a group of Australian investors in partnership with Falck of Italy, Siemens of Germany, and Clough Engineering, as well as Voest-Alpine of Austria. The proposed plant will use two Corex units, supplied by Voest-Alpine; an oxygen converter; and two thin-slab casters. The plant will require the construction of a power station, and this, in combination with the cost of the steel mill itself, will require an investment of Aus.$2.5 billion.

One of Australia's principal exports is iron ore. In 1991 Australia produced 123 million tonnes of ore, second only to Brazil, which produced 151 million tonnes. In terms of exports, in 1991, the Australian total was 113 million tonnes, second to Brazil with 114 million tonnes. In addition to developing ore mines, there has been a considerable amount of activity in terms of supplying the future Chinese industry, both with ore and direct-reduced iron. In western Australia, the government is backing a feasibility study to construct a direct-reduced-iron plant in the Pilbara region. The plant, if constructed, will be a joint venture with the Chinese. Its entire output will be sent to China, which has a 40 percent interest in the project.

In addition, Portman Mining signed an agreement with China's Anshan Iron and Steel Company, which would take an equity position of between 35–50 percent in the Koolyanobbing and Cockatoo Island iron ore projects, which would supply the Chinese company with considerable amounts of iron ore.

Republic of Korea

In 1967 when the government of the Republic of Korea began to think about building an integrated steel mill, production in the country stood at 300,000 tonnes, made basically in the obsolete open hearth. In a matter of twenty-five years, modern steel facilities have been built and production had grown to 33.0 million tonnes.

A consortium was put together in March 1967 and an agreement was signed among members of the Korean International Steel Associates which consisted of seven steel mill suppliers in four countries to pursue a study concerning the erection of an integrated steel plant. The original plant contemplated was to be constructed in two phases, the first with a capacity of 500,000 tonnes of raw steel and the second expanding capacity to 1 million tonnes. The proposal was submitted to the U.S. Export/Import Bank and the World Bank, both of which reached the conclusion that it was premature for Korea to have a steel mill. However, the Korean government decided to proceed with the project on its own.

Tae Joon Park, who had been president of the Korean Tungsten Mining Company, was made chairman of a promotion committee for the integrated steel mill. The size of the mill was expanded to 1 million tonnes for the first phase and financing was secured from Japan to erect the mill at Pohang, a village on the east coast of South Korea.

The first phase of the mill included a blast furnace, an oxygen converter, a battery of coke ovens, a slab mill, a plate mill, a billet mill, and a hot-strip mill, and was completed in 1973.

Thus, Korea had 1 million tonnes of steelmaking capacity in a single plant. Subsequently, Phases 2, 3, and 4 increased the capacity of the plant to 9.1 million tonnes. Later it was expanded to 9.4 million. The total cost of the mill, including the expansion to 9.4 million tonnes, was some $4 billion, somewhat in excess of $400 per tonne. The full construction was completed in 1981.

In the early 1980s there was considerable discussion concerning the construction of a second integrated steelworks. This was undertaken at Kwangyang, a location on the southern coast of the Republic of Korea. Construction actually began in early 1985 and continued rapidly, with the first phase completed in May 1987, representing a capacity of 2.7 million tonnes. The investment was approximately $1.8 billion. This phase included a sinter plant, a coke-oven battery, a blast furnace, a basic-oxygen shop, a continuous-cast caster, and hot- and cold-strip mills. Three phases followed before the mill was completed in 1992 with a capacity of 11.4 million tonnes, making it one of the world's largest. The investment for the entire Kwangyang plant was $8.2 billion, making the total investment for both plants $12.2 billion. Their total capacity is 21 million tonnes or $611 per tonne.

While this was in progress, a group of minimills operating electric furnaces rose up in the country with a total capacity in 1992 of between 11 and 12 million tonnes. There are some ten steelmaking companies in this group. The minimill companies and their capacities are listed in table 2–4. This sector has plans to increase its capacity to 16.4 million tonnes by 1995 with an investment of $3–$4 billion.

One of these mills, Hanbo, plans to enter the sheet business with the installation of a thin-slab caster and a hot-strip mill, with a total capacity of 1 million tonnes. Some of the other mills are currently examining the possibility of introducing a thin-slab caster, although no commitments have been made. Further plans by this group will expand its total capacity by the year 2000 to between 18 and 19 million tonnes.

Inchon Steel, one of the electric-furnace group, is investing

Table 2–4
South Korean Minimills

Company	Capacity (mil. of tonnes)
Inchon Iron & Steel	2.850
Dongkuk Steel Mill Co.	2.500
Hanbo Steel	1.000
Sammi Steel Co.	.800
Korean Iron & Steel Co.	1.580
Seoul Steel Co.	.150
Korea Heavy Industries	.240
Kai Steel	.180
Dae Han Steel Mill Co.	.240
Kangwon Industries	1.735

considerable sums in a modernization program that will increase its production to 3.5 million tonnes of raw steel. This will involve the installation of a 70-tonne electric furnace with a capacity for 500,000 tonnes per year, as well as an upgrading of the bar mill.

Dae Han Steel in Pusan will install a 50-tonne AC furnace that will add 20,000 tonnes per month to the company's capacity, virtually doubling the present figure. Union Steel is installing a new 100,000-tonne-per-year color sheet line that will double its present capacity at the Pusan works.

Pohang Iron and Steel plans to install an electric-furnace and thin-slab facilities at its Kwangyang plant, as well as a compact hot-strip mill with a 1-million-tonne capacity. The total cost of the project will be in excess of $400 million. Construction is to begin in mid-1995. The feed for the electric furnace will be quality scrap generated within the Kwangyang works, one of the largest integrated plants in the world, with a total capacity with the added mill, in excess of 12 million tonnes.

At the Pohang Works a Corex unit is now being installed that will produce 1,600 tonnes of iron a day or some 600,000 tonnes per year. Along with the Corex unit, which produces a very large quantity of gas, a power house will be built to convert this gas into electricity. Total investment will be close to $400 million. Thus, with the addition of Pohang's 1 million tonnes of sheets, the capacity of the Korean iron and steel industry will be about 40 million tonnes by the year 2000.

The steel industry in Korea has entered into a number of joint ventures outside the country. Perhaps the most significant one is with the United States division of USX in Pittsburg, California. The agreement was signed in 1986 and the joint-venture plant completed in 1989. It represented an investment of $500 million, shared on a 50-50 basis by the two partners. The plant included a six-high, cold-reduction mill for the production of cold-rolled sheets, as well as tinplate and galvanizing facilities.

The Korean steel industry also has investments in Southeast Asia. It is involved in a tinplate project in China with Shanghai No. 3 Iron and Steel Company, where a tinplate line with 120,000 tonnes of electrolytic capacity has been installed. POSCO has moved into Vietnam and Myanmar in Burma. In Vietnam, two new ventures were set up. In the first, POSCO and Kwanwon Industries agreed with VSC (Vietnam Steel Corporation) to form a 50-50 joint venture to construct a 200,000-tonne electric furnace to produce rebar and wire rod. The estimated investment is $100 million. In Myanmar, POSCO has formed a joint venture with Myanmar Metal Industries to operate a mill that will use rods to draw wire and cold-rolled sheets for galvanizing.

People's Republic of China

The steel industry in the People's Republic of China has had a remarkable growth in the past twelve years. In 1980, when production was 37 million tonnes, it was announced that by the year 2000 production would reach 100 million tonnes. Judging by the growth of the industry up to 1980, which had moved from 18 million tonnes in 1970 to 37 million tonnes in 1980, a production of 100 million tonnes by 2000 seemed impossible. However, in 1986, the Chinese steel industry passed the 52-million-tonne mark. From that point on, it grew rapidly to 80 million tonnes in 1992.

The world industry had not witnessed such growth since the

Japanese industry moved from 22 million tonnes to 93 million tonnes between the beginning and end of the 1960s. In fact, in 1992, the Chinese industry added another 10 million tonnes of output, moving from 71 million tonnes to 81 million tonnes.

As a consequence of this rapid increase, the goal of 100 million tonnes by the year 2000 seems to be readily obtainable, particularly in light of plans that have been made in the last few years to add three 10-million-tonne plants. These will be installed in phases of approximately 3 to 5 million tonnes each. Currently, the People's Republic of China ranks third in production among the steel-producing countries in the world, surpassed only by Japan and the United States.

During the next ten years the Chinese steel program intends to complete a number of projects that will add considerable tonnage and also replace some of the obsolete equipment the industry now operates. To produce 100 million tonnes, the Chinese industry will require iron ore imports to supplement the low-grade material that is available domestically. The average iron content of Chinese ore is approximately 34 percent. Iron ore imports of higher grade quality from the mid-1980s to 1990 averaged about 12 million tonnes annually. However, in 1991, ore imports increased to 19 million tonnes. To acquire necessary raw materials, China has looked to Australia and Peru. A study is underway in western Australia concerning the construction of a 2-million-tonne, direct-reduction-iron plant in the Pilbara region of Australia. The basis for the study is the projection that China will require almost 1 million tonnes of direct-reduced material by the end of the century. Pilbara has large supplies of high-grade iron ore as well as natural gas and suitable building sites, including those for ports and transport facilities. The study was organized by Western Australia's Department of Resource Development and the Chinese, with financing by the Western Australian-China Economic and Technology Research Fund.

China has also established a joint venture, the Sino-Australian Channar Mine, in western Australia. The mine went into operation in January 1990, and production has since increased each year. By 1998 output will be 10 million tonnes. The Chinese own 40 percent of the shares and Hammersley Iron PTY owns 60 percent. This joint venture is the first overseas iron ore venture for China. If all goes according to plans, over the next twenty years Channar Mine will produce 200 million tonnes of high-grade iron ore, all of which will be shipped to China.

In developing its steel industry during the 1980s, China erected a new integrated plant near Shanghai, known as Baoshan Steel Works. The plant is now in its third phase of construction. The third phase, consisting of the addition of 3 million tonnes of output, will involve a large blast furnace—indeed, one of the world's largest, with a daily production of 10,000 tonnes. The steelmaking facilities will consist of two 250-tonne oxygen converters that will bring the total sheet capacity of the plant to 10 million tonnes by 1998. There will also be an additional slab continuous caster and a semicontinuous hot-rolling mill, as well as a cold-rolling mill and provision for the production of 400,000 tonnes of tinplate.

Baoshan will ultimately control the steel mills in its territory from which eventually 600,000 tonnes will be exported, doubling the present export of 300,000 tonnes. There are further plans to construct an electric-arc furnace and a continuous caster to produce tube rounds. These will replace the existing slabbing and blooming mill that currently supplies Baoshan's seamless tube plant.

The three new integrated plants that are projected include the Zhanjang project. This plant is ultimately scheduled for a production of 10 million tonnes. However, the first phase, to be completed by the year 2000, will have 3 million tonnes of raw-steel capacity, which will be converted into flat-rolled products. This project is being financed by loans from the Guandong authorities. It is currently a 50–50 joint venture between Baoshan and Guandong, although outside investments would be welcome. The plant is to be located on deep water, capable of taking vessels with 250,000-tonne capacity, and will operate on ore supplied from overseas.

The second 10-million-tonne plant is a project of Shougang Steel, currently one of the largest producers in China. It is known as the Qi Lu project. Its first phase, which has been approved, will consist of a 5-million-tonne plant. The company already produces several million tonnes, and with the new plant ultimately expects to produce 20 million tonnes a year. The investment will come mainly from Shougang itself. The Chinese government and Shandong Province will also contribute, and hopefully so will some foreign investors. The facilities will come from the Shougang manufacturing segment, and from equipment purchased secondhand from outside China.

Shougang in the past has purchased a number of used and rebuilt steel mill facilities. In its current facility, the No. 2 Steel Plant consists of basic-oxygen converters and a slab caster, both of which were brought from Belgium. The steel shop produces 2.5 million tonnes, and it is projected that output will increase to 3 million tonnes. In addition to the steelmaking facilities, a wire-rod mill was also brought from Belgium. One of the company's recent acquisitions is an oxygen-converter plant that had stood idle at the California Steel Company for several years.

Shougang, in its manufacturing arm, produced a bar-rolling mill with an annual capacity of 100,000 tonnes for a steel company in Indonesia. The successful operation of this mill has brought many inquires from potential steel customers in Southeast Asia. Shougang plans to set up a joint venture in collaboration with Delhi-based Bahindcan to sell steel mill technology to the Indian mills. The company has also made an arrangement with the Jacinto Group of the Philippines to construct an integrated plant there. However, that plan has been put on hold.

The third large integrated plant scheduled for 10 million tonnes of output is the Bei Hai project in Chianghai Province.

In addition to these three large integrated plants, there is another project, under the aegis of Baoshan, that will be constructed at Ningbo, south of Shanghai. The project is on a relatively small-scale, with the first phase consisting of a 1.5-

million-tonne plant for the production of sheet and strip. This will be completed by the year 2000 and subsequently expanded to 3 million tonnes. It will be the second mill in China to use direct reduction as a means of procuring iron.

In another area, China's largest steelmaker, Anshan Iron and Steel, is currently planning to increase its production to 10 million tonnes by the mid-1990s. The plant operates seven blast furnaces and also operates a significant amount of what could be considered obsolete equipment, much of which will have to be replaced. At the present time, much of its steel is made by the open hearth. Ultimately, this will be replaced by oxygen converters, hopefully by the mid-1990s.

The People's Republic of China also will construct a number of thin-slab casters and minimills. One such plant is the Zhujiang project, a joint venture with Italy's Falck and other partners. Production from this thin-slab caster will be in excess of 800,000 tonnes a year; its facilities will include an electric furnace, a thin-slab caster, and a hot- and cold-strip mill.

Investment is being made in China by several steelmakers located outside the country. One of these is Kawasaki Steel of Japan, which will build a silicon electric-sheet processing plant. It will process about 1,000 tonnes a month of silicon sheets, which will be shipped from Kawasaki in Japan.

Another company from a foreign country, Hanbo Steel of South Korea, intends to build a large minimill in China to make reinforcing bars. The mill will produce some 700,000 tonnes a year in the Tianjin industry zone. The arrangement will be a 50–50 partnership between Hanbo and its Chinese partners. The possibility has been considered of expanding capacity from 700,000 tonnes to 1 million tonnes within a short time.

The Japanese minimill company Toyo Steel Manufacturing has made a direct investment in production facilities in China. Recently, the company formed a joint venture with Shenyang Steel Rolling General Mill. The project will result in a new plant to produce 240,000 tonnes of billets. The new company, to be known as Shenyang Toyo Steel, will be owned 60 percent by

Toyo and 40 percent by Shenyang. A 40-tonne electric furnace and a billet caster will be installed.

Maanshan Steel Company recently placed an order for a conventional slab-casting machine that will enable it to cast slabs for 700,000 tonnes of plate production. This output is to be expanded in the coming years to 2 million tonnes.

The plan to produce 100 million tonnes by the year 2000 will result in a large amount of steel. However, it is still far less than the 100kg per capita that is the consumption level of developed countries. But this new plan is suitable for Chinese conditions. The reasons given are:

1. China is going to be a modernized country. However, the demand for steel production is huge in the domestic market.
2. When we consider the domestic market in China, we must also look at the domestic rural market. There lives 800 million people. Actual consumption of steel per capita is even less than the figure in the city. The development of the rural market will boost additional demand for steel.
3. Attention must also be paid to the change of structure in the future market, for example, the car industry is just unfolding in China. Following the development of the car industry, road construction, car parking, service stations, and also traffic control systems must be set up. The demand for steel production is going to be very encouraging.[4]

India

India's crude steel output increased from 14 million tonnes in 1989 to 18 million tonnes in 1992. Hopes for the future were expressed at a conference in Bombay in late 1992, when Mr. Santosh Mohan Dev, the steel minister, assessed India's potential to become one of the world's leaders in steel operations. He asserted that the current 18-million-tonne figure could be raised to 67 million tonnes by the year 2010. Such an increase would raise the level of per capita consumption from the present 26kg, which is one of the lowest in the world, to 65kg by 2010. This rapid increase in a matter of seventeen years would be most unusual when one considers that during the past twenty years India's steel production rose from 6.8 million tonnes in 1972 to the current 18-million-tonne figure in 1992. The optimism that prompted this projected expansion was due principally to a change in government policy toward business in general and to steel operations in particular.

In a document produced by a task force on the growth plan for the steel industry up to 2012, a list of the possible steel plants to be constructed by 2012 is given. However, the document includes a definite caveat. The report states:

> The probable sites as well as the capacities assumed are based on planning documents, investment decisions taken by existing steel plants and investment initiatives taken by new entrepreneurs. There are also proposals for a large number of small plants of capacity less than 0.5 Mt, some of which are already in various stages of implementation.
>
> All the projects however may not materialize. Even allowing for likely mortality, achieving a capacity of 67 Mt of crude steel (equivalent to 57 Mt of finished steel) seems realistic and reasonable too.

The list proposed by the task force spreads the future capacity of the plants in question over a period of twenty years, which are divided into four plans: Plan VIII: 1996–97, Plan IX: 2001–2, Plan X: 2006–7, and Plan XI: 2011–12. In addition to providing the possible steel plants to be constructed, the task force report also details the raw materials needed to service these plants, which reach large proportions, particularly in respect to iron ore and coking coal.

The possible plants, whose capacity would add up to 67 million tonnes, are listed with their individual capacities installed over a period of twenty years, and the report also details their geographic locations in terms of the state in which they will be constructed (see table 2–5).

The extensive growth in India's steel industry outlined in the task force plan may well not be achieved. However, as the re-

Table 2–5
India: Plans to Expand Steel Capacity
(in million tonnes)

No.	Location/Organization	VIII Plan	IX Plan	X Plan	XI Plan	State
1	SAIL[b]	12.5	16.0	19.0	24.0	
2	TISCO	3.1	3.1	5.0	5.0	Bihar
3	RINL[b]	3.0	4.5	6.0	9.0	AP
4	ESSAR STEEL	1.8	1.8	1.8	1.8	Gujrat
5	DAITARI (1)	1.0	1.0	3.0	3.0	Orissa
6	NINL, DAITARI	—	1.0	1.0	3.0	Orissa
7	DAITARI (2)	—	1.0	1.0	3.0	Orissa
8	HOSPET	—	1.7	2.8	3.0	Karnataka
9	BAILADILA	—	1.5	2.0	3.0	M.P
10	MANGALORE	—	1.5	1.5	3.0	Karnataka
11	MORMUGAO	—	1.0	2.0	3.0	Goa
12	MANOHARPUR	—	1.6	3.0	3.0	Bihar
13	SURJAGARH	—	—	1.5	3.0	Maharashtra
14	ALIBAG	—	1.0	2.0	2.0	Maharashtra
15	KAKINADA[a]	—	1.0	2.0	3.0	A.P
16	GUNA/JAGDISHP UR[a]	—	—	1.0	2.0	MP/UP
17	PIPAVA/VAGARA	—	—	1.0	2.0	Gujrat
18	HALDIA	—	—	1.5	3.0	W.B
19	SALEM	—	—	—	1.5	Tamilnadu
20	RAIGARH/RATNAGIRI	—	—	1.0	3.0	MP/Maharastra
21	ONGOLE	—	—	—	1.0	A.P
22	KARWAR	—	—	—	2.0	Karnataka
23	PONDICHERRY/ CUDDALORE	—	—	—	1.0	Pondicherry
24	NE REGION	—	—	—	1.0	
25	OTHER SECONDARY UNITS	7.5	9.0	10.5	12.0	

[a] Subject to availability of gas.

[b] Projections only.

port says, achieving a major portion of this planned growth will go a long way toward producing the 67 million tonnes of crude steel India hopes to generate.

The materials needed to service these tonnages are listed in table 2–6.

The largest steel company in India is SAIL, which represents five integrated plants and had a production of 9.9 million tonnes of steel in 1992. Its plans for the future call for 16 million tonnes by 2001 and 24 million tonnes by 2012. Since SAIL is the largest single producer in India, if it manages to reach its goal of 24 million tonnes by 2012 it by itself would contribute more than one-third to India's national goal. However, more plants would have to be built to realize half of the 67 million tonnes projected as a possibility by the minister of steel.

A large number of new Indian steel plants have been proposed, some of which are currently under construction and a significant portion of which are still in the planning and discussion stages. The government's latest plant, Visakhaphenam, which is referred to as VIZAG, was completed and dedicated in the latter part of 1992. It was very costly to build because of frequent delays. The government has announced that it will not invest in any new integrated steel plants; thus the integrated segment of the business is totally dependent for investment on entrepreneurs from the private sector. As a consequence, a number of new possibilities have sprung up and are in the discussion stage.

These include a plant at Essar with 2 million tonnes of hot-rolled-coil facilities. Essar has also established a plant to make over 1 million tonnes of direct-reduced iron (DRI) as well as a 2-million-tonne pellet plant. This company has been successful in selling DRI in the export market, exporting more than 200,000 tonnes of it in the early months of 1993. The company's two plants for producing DRI were imported second-hand from Germany. The rated capacity of these two plants is now 1.3 million tonnes.

ESSAR Gujarat plans to build a new 2-million-tonne plant that will produce hot-rolled coil and plate. This will be located on the same site as its Midrex iron modular. The company plans to produce strip and sheet of deep-drawing quality for the au-

Table 2–6
Demand for Raw Materials for India's Steel Growth
(millions of tonnes)

Raw Materials	1996–97	2001–2	2006–7	2011–12
Iron ore	50	68	93	126
Coking coal including import (landed)	41	46	57	74
Noncoking coal	5	12	16	21
Limestone & dolomite	14	18	25	34

tomotive industry as well as other consumers. The new plant will have three 150-tonne electric furnaces, a conventional slab caster, and a hot-strip mill to be supplied by European mill builders.

Another steel plant with a capacity in excess of 1 million tonnes is proposed by Bhushan Steel and Strip Company which has an agreement with Voest-Alpine of Austria to install a Corex unit with some 650,000 tonnes of capacity that will be part of a new integrated mill to be built at Daitari in Orissa. Currently, the company operates an electric-arc steelmaking plant, producing steel structural sections.

Another proposal has been made by the Jindal Iron and Steel Company, which is attempting to expand its slab-making capacity to 300,000 tonnes, as well as its coil capacity to 200,000 tonnes from 150,000 tonnes. It is also planning a galvanizing plant and a 60,000-tonne plant for coal-based sponge iron. This group has recently installed a pipe mill bought second-hand from the United States. Most important of all the Jindal projects is the possibility of a 2-million-tonne hot-strip mill.

There is also the possibility that two new steel mills, each with 1 million tonnes of capacity, could be built at Bijayanagar, in the south of India. These steel works have been under discussion for many years.

Lloyd's Steel Industries is preparing a site near Nagpur for a hot-strip mill. The first phase will produce 400,000 tonnes. This mill will be fed from an electric-arc furnace and is expected to come on line in April 1994. The second phase will involve cold-rolled facilities to be commissioned in late 1994. The company has also started work on a 300,000-tonne sponge-iron plant.

This will be the third hot-strip mill to be installed within the last two years. The first was at Tata's plant and the second, a 2-million-tonne mill, is currently under construction at Essar Gutjarat. The Lloyd plant will be using a secondhand steckel mill.

Table 2–7 offers a second list of new proposed steel plants and provides more detail in terms of the companies involved;

the document to create table 2–7 was received from India's Ministry of Steel.

Upgrading Facilities. One of the principal projects in India is the upgrading of existing steel facilities. In fact, many have suggested that this be undertaken prior to the erection of new facilities. The clearance has been given to SAIL to upgrade its Bokaro steel plant. The plan is to call for tenders from around the world. Phase 1 of the upgrading involves the introduction of continuous casting as well as a modernization of the melt shop and the hot-rolling mill.

At another SAIL plant, at Durgapur, there has been considerable upgrading, including the erection of a blast furnace and the modernization of a number of units. Durgapur was expanded to a crude steel capacity of 1.6 million tonnes. However, this capacity has yet to be fully utilized. Oxygen converters are being installed as well as continuous casting. A third plant in the SAIL group, Burnpur, is being considered for privatization.

Part of India's steelmaking capacity consists of a number of minimills, which totaled 175 in 1991. Many of these minimills are quite small, with electric furnaces having a heat size of 5–10 tonnes. In fact, the majority have a furnace size with less than 10 tonnes per heat. In 1992 these electric-furnace operations contributed 28 percent of the 18.1 million tonnes of Indian steel production, or 4.6 million tonnes. Some 100 of the 175 furnaces were recently closed down because of the rise in scrap prices of 40 percent which reached as high as $180 a tonne.

As a means of solving the scrap problem, India is installing a large tonnage of direct-reduced iron (DRI). This process began in the 1980s with the installation of six units with a total of 600,000 tonnes. In the early 1990s eleven more units were installed; as of 1993 they are operating with a capacity of 1.9 million tonnes. In late 1993, there were under construction or in the planning stage eight units with a total capacity of 2.4 million tonnes. This provides a possible total capacity, both from those in operation and those under construction, of 4.9 million tonnes

Table 2–7
New Proposed Steel Plants in India

No.	Name	Item	Equivalent Steel Capacity in M TPA	Production Year
1.	Lloyd's Steel Industries Ltd.	EAF	0.44	94–95, 94 Apr
2.	Essar Gujarat Ltd.	EAF	1.76	94–95, 94 Oct
3.	Jindal Strips Ltd (at Raigarh)	EAF	0.55	95–96, 95 Dec
4.	Malvika Steel Products	BOF	0.30	94–95, 94 Dec
5.	Mideast Integrated Steels Ltd.	BOF	0.55	95–96, 95 Sep
6.	Nippon Denro Ispat Ltd.	EAF	1.32	95–96, 95 Sep
7.	Malvika Steel Products Ltd.	BOF	0.30	95–96, 96 Jan
8.	Nilachal Ispat Nigam Ltd.	BOF	1.05	97–98, 97 Dec
9.	Jindal Iron & Steel (Vijaynagar)	BOF	1.29	95–96, 95 Sep
10.	Arm Steel Plant	BOF	0.36	95–96, 96 Mar
11.	Jaiprakash Engg. & Steel Co. Ltd	BOF	1.10	96–97
12.	Jaiprakash Engg. & Steel Co. Ltd.	BOF	0.60	97–98
13.	Kalinga Steels (India) Ltd.	BOF	1.65	97–98, 97 End
14.	Vijayanagar - 1 Project	BOF	1.10	97–98, Not firm
15.	Mukand Ltd.	BOF	1.20	98–99, Not firm
16.	Orind Steels Ltd.	BOF	1.15	Not indicated
17.	JK Industries Ltd.	BOF	0.60	Not indicated
18.	Birla Technical Services	EAF	0.80	Not indicated
19.	Arm Steel Plant	BOF	1.10	Not indicated
20.	Sathavahana Ispat Ltd.	P	0.12	
21.	Lanco Ferro Ltd.	P	0.1	
22.	Suryavanshi Steels & Alloys	P	0.13	
23.	Tata Kothari Steels Ltd.	P S-BOF	0.12	
24.	Kumar's Metallurgical Ltd.	DR C	0.06	
25.	Midwest Iron & Steel	P	0.07	
26.	Asian Mineral Industries	P	0.23	
27.	Arm Steel Plant	S-BOF	1.10	
28.	Arm Steel Plant	S-BOF	1.10	
29.	Auroma Coke Manufacturers	C	0.1	
30.	Shree Gagdamba Beneficiation	C	0.1	
31.	MK Coke Industries Pvt. Ltd.	C	0.1	
32.	Usha Martin Industries Ltd.	P	0.11	
33.	Punjab Steel Products Ltd.	S-BOF	0.36	
34.	Punjab Steel Products Ltd.	S-BOF	0.69	
35.	Bihar Sponge Iron Ltd. (Expan)	DR C	0.15	
36.	Essar Gujarat Ltd.	S-EAF	1.76	
37.	Sesa Goa Ltd.	P	0.08	
38.	Nova Dhatu Udyog Ltd.	P	0.08	
39.	Sandur Manganese & Iron Ores	C	0.06	
40.	Uni Metal Ispat Ltd.	P	0.07	
41.	Vijayanagar - 1 Project	S-BOF	1.10	
42.	Jindal Iron & Steel Ltd.	S-BOF	1.29	
43.	Jaiprakash Engg. & Steel Co. Ltd.	S-BOF	0.60	
44.	Jaiprakash Engg. & Steel Co. Ltd.	S-BOF	0.60	

Table 2–7 (Continued)
New Proposed Steel Plants in India

No.	Name	Item	Equivalent Steel Capacity in M TPA	Production Year
45.	Kirloskar Ferrous Industries	P	0.12	
46.	Nippon Denro Ispat Ltd.	S-EAF	1.32	
47.	Sunflag Iron & Steel (Expan)	DR C	0.15	
48.	Nippon Denro Ispat Ltd.	DR G	1.00	
49.	Kalyani Steels Ltd.	DR G	0.60	
50.	Usha Ispat Ltd.	P S-BOF	0.10	
51.	Usha Ispat Ltd.	P S-BOF	0.10	
52.	Lloyds Steels Industries Ltd.	S-EAF	0.44	
53.	Om Iron & Steel Industries Ltd.	P	0.40	
54.	Mukand Ltd.	S-BOF	1.20	
55.	Prakash Industries Ltd.	DR C	0.15	
56.	Nova Steel	DR C	0.15	
57.	Jindal Strips Ltd.	S-EAF	0.55	
58.	Nagpur Alloy Castings Ltd.	P S-BOF	0.32	
59.	JK Industries Ltd.	O S	0.23	
60.	Raipur Steel & Alloy Ltd.	DR C	0.06	
61.	Monnet Ispat Ltd.	DR C	0.10	
62.	Vandana Rolling Mills	DR C	0.15	
63.	JK Industries Ltd.	S-BOF	0.60	
64.	Nagpur Engg. Co. (NECO)	C	0.12	
65.	IDC of Orissa (IDCOL)	C	0.12	
66.	Kalinga Steels (India) Ltd.	S-BOF	1.65	
67.	Nilachal Ispat Nigam Ltd.	S-BOF	1.05	
68.	Powmex Ispat Ltd.	P	0.64	
69.	Mideast Integrated Steel Ltd.	S-BOF	0.55	
70.	Orind Steels Ltd.	S-BOF	1.15	
71.	Southern Iron & Steel Co. Ltd.	P S-BOF	0.18	
72.	Tamilnadu Sponge Ltd.	DR C	0.03	
73.	Southern Iron & Steel Co. Ltd.	P S-BOF	0.36	
74.	Malvika Steel Products Ltd.	S-BOF	0.29	
75.	Malvika Steel Products Ltd.	S-BOF	0.50	
76.	Malvika Steel Products Ltd.	DR G	0.29	
77.	Birla Technical Services	P S	0.57	
78.	Tata Metaliks Ltd.	P	0.09	
79.	Century Textiles & Industries	P	0.30	
80.	Birla Technical Services	S-EAF	0.80	

P = Pig Iron, PS BOF = Pig Iron (Steel Production Later Date) S(BOF) = Steel (BF-BOF Route), SEAF = Steel (EAF Route) C = Coke Oven.

of DRI. This will be a supplement or, in some places, a complete replacement of scrap for the electric furnaces.

India expects to increase its production of DRI by several million tonnes by the year 2000. One of these plants, namely, that constructed by Nippon, Denro Ispat Ltd., a privately-owned corporation headquartered in Calcutta, is in the process of building a 1-million-tonne hot-briquetted-iron plant near Dharamtar in Maharastara State. The plant will produce hot-briquetted iron for use in electric-arc furnaces for the production of steel. The investment required is $44.8 million, of which the U.S. Export-Import Bank will loan $39.7 million. Repayment will be made in twenty semiannual installments beginning in May 1995.

India's hope of achieving a capacity of 67 million tonnes by 2012 has been brought on by changes in government policy in relation to business in general and steel specifically. Previous government policies that demanded licenses were restrictive in terms of permitting expansion. Delicensing will have an effect in terms of permitting additional capacity in steel, and so too will new government rules allowing very significant foreign investment.

Brazil

Steel in Brazil has witnessed considerable growth since 1970. At that time, production was 5.4 million tonnes. By 1980, output had grown to 13.9 million tonnes. By 1985, it had increased to 20.5 million tonnes. Output reached its peak in 1989 with production of 25.1 million tonnes. Since that time, it has declined slightly but regained 25.1 million tonnes in 1993.

In the late 1980s the large steel plants were owned by the Brazilian government and others by private entrepreneurs. The Brazilian government owned the integrated plants based on blast-furnace output and announced, at that time, an ambitious plan to raise the total steel output in Brazil to 50 million tonnes by the year 2000. The government plants planned to spend some $11 billion on expansion and development to accomplish this goal. Brazil was also active in exports, having increased its exports from 2.4 million tonnes in 1982 to 10.9 million tonnes in 1991.

The decision to privatize the industry affected expansion plans. Now that privatization has been completed, there are very few plans for expansion among the integrated companies. It appears that by the year 2000 Brazil will probably have a production of about 30 million tonnes. Currently, Brazil ranks ninth among the steel producers of the world.

On October 24, 1991, Usiminas was the first of the government-owned companies to be privatized. The selling price was $1.17 billion, which was provided by a number of interested parties. CVRD, the state-owned iron ore company, purchased 15 percent of the shares and its pension plan purchased another 7 percent. One of the pension funds of a government bank purchased 15 percent, thereby giving two government-owned agencies 37 percent of the shares. A group of ten other investors joined together to purchase 50.49 percent of the voting shares. One of the largest was Nippon-Usiminas with 14 percent. Another was a group of Usiminas employees with a 10 percent share. Others with smaller percentages make up the total 50.49 percent. The total price of $1.17 billion was 14 percent higher than the minimum price of $1.08 billion set by the government.

Among the government-owned plants was Tuberao Steel Company, referred to as CST. It began operations in November 1983 with a capacity to produce some 3 million tonnes of ingot-cast slabs. Originally, it was owned 24 percent by Kawasaki, 24 percent by Ilva, and 52 percent by the Brazilian government. This joint venture was designed so that both Kawasaki and Ilva would take a share of the output commensurate with their ownership shares, while the balance would be sold in Brazil. However, in 1982, because of the worldwide recession in the steel industry, the original plan was changed and the entire production of CST was put up for sale. One shortcoming of the 3 million tonnes of slabs produced per year at CST was the lack of a continuous caster.

In the late 1980s when the Brazilian government decided to double the capacity of its integrated steel mills, it was anticipated that by the year 2000 CST's production would be 6 million tonnes, part of which was to be rolled into hot-rolled coils for sale, another part of which was to be continuously-cast strip-mill slabs, and the remainder was to be ingots reduced on the slabbing mill for plate slabs. When privatization took place in August 1992, 89 percent of the stock was purchased by two Brazilian banks and a Brazilian mining company and the employees, with 11 percent still held jointly by Ilva and Kawasaki, each with 5.5 percent.

At present, the plan to double the size of CST has been dropped. Current plans call for the installation of a continuous caster that will form 2 million tonnes of slabs with thicknesses of 8, 9, and 10 inches. The remaining steel, approximately 1.2 million tonnes, will be rolled into slabs on the slabbing mill and will be sold primarily to plate mills. Thus, CST will produce continuously-cast slabs for the strip mills of the world and slabs from ingots for plate mills also on a worldwide basis. The market for slabs is increasing in most steel-producing countries so that there should be no difficulty in disposing of CST's full output.

Cosipa was the last of the fully integrated government-owned plants to be privatized. The actual auction of its stock took place on August 20, 1993. The group that purchased it was made up principally of steel distributors led by Marcus de Araujo Tambascu, who represented Brastubo. The total amount invested in the stock was $331 million, almost double the minimum auction price set by the company in its privatization effort. Brastubo in league with several other distributors purchased 69 percent of Cosipa's voting shares. Another group of distributors failed in their bid. Some 4.9 percent was acquired by another group, including CVRD, as well as Cosipa's employees. An additional 15 percent has been reserved for sale to the company's employees. Brastubo's share of the stock was 57.4 percent. Several days after purchasing this amount, the management of Brastubo sought a partner with steel mill experience. Usiminas, the first company privatized, responded to Brastubo's request and purchased 49.79 percent of Cosipa's ordinary capital for approximately $200 million.

CSN, the largest integrated steel company in Brazil, was sold at auction on May 2, 1993. Of the stock, 51 percent, a controlling share, was purchased by a consortium composed of CVRD, an ore company, a bank, a textile group, and a steel trader, as well as CSN employees. Foreign investors took 2.3 percent. The employee group purchased 20 percent and the pension fund 10.9 percent. Total investment was $1.1 billion. The company plans to invest another $800 million over the next few years, principally to break bottlenecks in its production sequence. It has been estimated that production will increase from 4.5 million to 6 million tonnes.

On November 15, 1991, the government put one of its minimills, Cosinor, up for sale at a minimum price of $12.8 million. The Gerdau Group, the largest minimill organization in Brazil, bought it for $14.3 million. For this amount, Gerdau acquired 89.9 percent of the voting shares.

In February 1992 a government-owned, semi-integrated plant, Piratini, was sold to the Gerdau Group for $107 million, which purchased 89.29 percent of the stock. It also accepted a $24 million debt and a $10 million obligation owed to the workers. Further, it agreed to spend $30 million to modernize the mill. Thus, the total cost to the Gerdau interest was $171 million.

Future Investment in Brazilian Steel. Much of the investment that will be made in Brazil to expand capacity will be made by the minimill group. The fully-integrated group, recently purchased in the privatization move, will be spending very little money on expansion. Most of their investment will be for modernization and reduction of costs. This is a complete reversal from the announcement made in 1989 by Siderbras, the overall holding company for the government-owned mills. It was stated then that a total amount of $11 billion was needed for steel investment to modernize the government's plants. Of this total, $1.46 billion was assigned to Usiminas which would increase its capacity slightly to bring its rate of continuous casting up to 100 percent. Now that the industry is in private hands and no longer can count on government funds, investment to increase capacity will be made sparingly. In fact, it is doubtful that the industry in Brazil will add more than 8–10 million tonnes to its capacity by the turn of the century.

Brazil will continue to export large amounts of steel, probably over 40 percent of its production. It will also continue to be the world's largest supplier of iron ore through CVRD, the government-owned ore company. As an exporter of considerable tonnage of steel—almost 12 million tonnes—it will be in competition with the industrialized countries of the world, particularly Japan and those in Western Europe. The tonnage of exports will continue to increase. In 1992, it reached 12 million tonnes, or 54 percent of steel output. Brazil will remain a formidable player in the world steel industry with its exports of steel and iron ore.

In 1986, at a meeting of ILAFA, the president of the institute, Cesar Mendoza, spoke of the need to increase the capacity of the Latin American steel industry. The argument advanced was that Latin America's per capita consumption of crude steel should rise from the level in 1984 of 75kg to at least the world average of 150kg. Mendoza noted that to improve the living standards of Latin America's growing population, crude steel production must be raised. Mendoza called for an increase of 6 million tonnes. At that time, Latin American production was 35.8 million tonnes. Output rose to an all-time high of 42.4 million tonnes in 1989, after which it declined somewhat to the upper 30-million-tonne range. However, in 1992, it recovered to 41.1 million tonnes. Thus, the needs Mendoza projected in 1986 were fulfilled. Not much more growth can be expected in the remaining years of the decade. The steel industry in Brazil will improve its quality and reduce its cost through judicious investment.

In what used to be Brazil's private sector before the privatization of the government's steel works, the Gerdau group was the largest operation. Recently, it closed a 500,000-tonne-per-year blast furnace at its Santa Cruz works because of high charcoal prices. The furnace will be removed to a plant in Minas Gerais to replace obsolete facilities. It will operate there on a 50-50 charcoal/coke basis.

At the plant in Barao de Cocais in Minias Gerais, a new bar-mill facility, capable of producing 120,000 tonnes per year, will be installed to absorb the excess billet capacity that now exists at that plant. The blast furnace at Barao de Cocais will supply pig iron for the Santa Cruz works, in conjunction with another 600,000-tonne-per-year furnace at the same plant.

At the Santa Cruz plant, there are plans to install a bar-and-rod mill. Some $16 million will be spent on environmental controls. This is the largest plant in the Gerdau Group with some 900,000 tonnes per year, while the plant in Minas Gerais produces 240,000 tonnes per year.

Taiwan

Taiwan has witnessed a remarkable growth in steel output during the last twenty-five years. In 1969 Taiwan's production was 480,000 tonnes. By 1975, output had risen to 1 million tonnes. By 1980, output had increased to 3.4 million tonnes, and in 1992 production was 10.8 million tonnes. Taiwan's steel consumption in 1992 was almost 18 million tonnes, which included imports of 8.8 million tonnes. Exports were 2.1 million tonnes, making Taiwan the second largest net importer in the world. The growth in production has been due principally to the expansion of its steel company, China Steel, an integrated steel operation, of some 5.4 million tonnes during the 1980s.

Future plans for Taiwan include an attempt to become independent of imports by the year 2000. China Steel is currently in its fourth phase of development, during which it will add 2.4 million tonnes of output at a total cost of $2.5 billion. It is hoped that this fourth phase will be completed by mid-1997. This will be the final expansion of the company's plant at its current site. The project will include a fourth blast furnace, additional steel-making facilities, and a second hot-strip mill that will increase China Steel's capacity to 8 million tonnes.

In the late 1980s An Feng Steel Company installed a hot-strip mill with a capacity to produce 2 million tonnes. Since An Feng did not produce steel, the mill depended on slab imports. Recently, An Feng has signed an agreement to construct a mill for the production of rebars; initially this mill will depend on imported billets from the Philippines. The company has also made plans to build a 5-million-tonne integrated plant. Stage 1 of the plant, with 2 million tonnes of capacity, will be completed in 1996. Stage 2 will increase capacity by 3 million tonnes, but to some extent will be dependent on export potential to China. The mill will probably be based on the Corex process, as well as the direct-reduction process for the production of iron, and will use energy-optimizing furnaces for the production of steel. The total investment for stage 1 will be just short of $1 billion.

In addition to the An Feng plant, the Yieh Loong Steel Group has announced a project to build an integrated steel plant with a 6.5-million-tonne capacity. The project will be constructed over a period of five years at a cost of $3.9 billion. It will include a hot-strip mill, a plate mill, and a structural mill. It may also include the production of slabs, badly needed in a country that now imports some 7.5 million tonnes of this product.

Several lesser but important developments are taking place in the steel industry in Taiwan. Tung Ho has just completed Taiwan's first H-beam steel plant, with a capacity of 500,000 tonnes. Tang Eng, a stainless steel producer, has installed a new Zendzimir mill for cold rolling with a 200,000-tonne capacity. It has also added a 40-tonne, electric-arc furnace as well as a ladle furnace that will add 100,000 tonnes to its capacity, bringing the total to 300,000 tonnes. Another stainless producer, Mung Development Company, has arranged to install two Zendzimir mills at its new plant, which should be in operation in early 1994. This is a joint venture with Krupp Stahl of Germany. Another minimill, Hai Kwang Enterprise, has bought a new bar mill.

Taiwan will rank high among the steel-producing countries of the world with the addition of 14 million tonnes of capacity in the next few years. However, Taiwan will continue to depend on imported iron ore.

Southeast Asia

The steel industry in Southeast Asia was very small in the 1970s but has grown significantly through 1992. The principal steel-producing countries of Southeast Asia are Indonesia, Malaysia, and Thailand. In 1980 steel production in Indonesia was 543,000 tonnes; by 1992, Indonesia's output had grown to 3.1 million tonnes. Thailand had a production of 450,000 tonnes in 1980, which increased to 1.2 million tonnes by 1992. Malaysia's production in 1980 was 210,000 tonnes which grew significantly to an estimated 1.5 million tonnes by 1992. The increase in these countries came principally from joint ventures carried out with companies in Japan, Korea, and Taiwan.

Projected growth in this area of the world to the year 2000 is significant. Judging by the number of projects that are either under construction or in the planning stage, total capacity for steel production in these three countries could amount to 10–12 million tonnes by the year 2000. The 1992 figure totaled approximately 6 million tonnes. A review of some of the projects that are either underway or in the planning stage will illustrate the area's potential for growth.

Thailand. There is currently a shortage of bars in Thailand and, as a consequence, production is supplemented heavily by imports. Six mills have been given licenses to produce steel bars, but only three are under construction. Consequently, the government has been encouraged to grant more licenses for the construction of steel operations.

Thailand, with the help of Nippon Steel of Japan, is planning an H-beam mill with a capacity of 800,000 tonnes a year. It will be a minimill requiring an investment of some $40 million for the roughing and finishing stands. Steel will be provided by a 120-tonne electric-arc furnace and by a 120-tonne ladle furnace to feed a continuous-casting beam-blank mill as well as a rolling mill to make the finished product. Several interests are involved, including Siam Steel and Yamato Kogyo of Japan. This will be the first H-beam mill in Thailand.

Sumitomo Metal Industries of Japan is investing in the construction of a pipe mill for electric welded pipe. The facility will be installed at Thai Steel Pipe Company, south of Bangkok. Sumitomo owns 50 percent of Thai Steel Pipe Company; Nomura Trading owns 25 percent; and Mitsui and Siam Steel Pipe each own 12½ percent of the company. The line will have a capacity at 400 tonnes per month to meet the demand of the automobile industry.

The Sahaviriya Group in Thailand has a new hot-strip mill under construction. It is a joint venture between Thai investors and Italian partners, including Duferco Trading Company and Iretecna, formerly known as Italimpianti; the latter has supplied the mill equipment. The hot-strip mill will not have a source of steel on the premises, and therefore will need to import approximately 2 million tonnes of slabs to feed it. Sahaviriya Steel Industries is studying the possibility of installing a cold-strip mill. The same group is also building a galvanizing line in conjunction with other investors such as NKK, Marubeni, and Itochu of Japan. The hot-strip mill will require an investment of several hundred million dollars. The projected investment for the cold mill is also several hundred million. The new galvanizing line will require an investment of $120 million.

Thailand is venturing into the electrolytic-galvanizing field with a plant to be in operation by early 1994. Partners in this project are Japan's NKK and Marubeni, who own 60 percent of the venture, and Thai Coated Sheet Company, which owns 40 percent. Capacity is scheduled for 135,000 tonnes.

Other projects which are underway in Thailand include those that are also joint ventures with the Japanese. There are a number of these involved in the finishing end of the steel business. They include two tinplate projects which will increase the capacity of the country to produce tinplate by approximately half a million tonnes, and four galvanizing steel projects financed by separate companies including Thai Coated Steel Sheet, Far East Iron Works, Sangkai Thai, and Bangkok Steel Industry, totaling some 400,000 tonnes of galvanized steel. The Japanese partners include Marubeni, Mitsui, Kobe, and Nisshio Iwai.

Malaysia. Malaysia's steel production has grown sevenfold since 1980 and is now estimated to be 1.5 million tonnes. One of the largest projects in Southeast Asia was decided for Malaysia with the participation of China Steel of Taiwan. It was to be a 2-million-tonne integrated plant in its first phase, and was ultimately to be expanded to 5 million tonnes. Unfortunately, the arrangement with China Steel was terminated so that the proposed plant has been abandoned.

Since the termination of this project, there has been considerable activity in Malaysia directed at installing a hot-strip mill for the production of flat-rolled steel products. Three companies, Amalgamated Steel Mills (ASM), a division of the Lion's Group; Perwaja, which is involved in steel operations; and Nusantara Steel Corporation, are making definite plans to build a mill, but as yet none of the three has made a definite start.

The first group, ASM, plans to install a 5.4-million-tonne Megasteel project. This is to be constructed in three phases, the first of which will be capable of producing 1.8 million tonnes; this plant is expected to be in operation by the end of 1995 or early 1996. It will consist of two 150-tonne DC electric furnaces, two ladle furnaces, two vacuum degassers, two thin-slab casters, and a compact hot-strip mill. The company is negotiating for a site in Malaysia. The capital investment will be in the area of $1 billion. It is expected that the plant will export some 30 percent of its output.

Perwaja, the second group, has been granted a license by the

Malaysian Ministry of International Trade and Industry to build and operate a thin-slab caster with an accompanying minimill to produce sheets. At first, the prospective partners in the project were Nippon Steel of Japan and Nucor of the United States. The plant was to have a 1.5-million-tonne-capacity mill, and was planned to be in operation by the end of 1996. The administration at Perwaja had second thoughts concerning the thin-slab caster, since its product, which would be made from electric-furnace steel based on scrap with a proportion of direct-reduced iron (DRI), would not be able to serve the full range of applications, particularly the automotive grades. The general manager of Perwaja has stated that he requires a slab three to four inches thick and will be deciding on technology that may not include a thin-slab caster. Consequently, Nucor would not be involved in any partnership, since the thin-slab caster will more than likely be abandoned. Therefore, the administration at Perwaja is seeking a partner in Japan to help it with funding. Conversations have been held with the principal Japanese companies including Nippon Steel, NKK, and Kawasaki.

The flat-rolled-products market in Malaysia rose to 2 million tonnes in 1993 and is projected to reach 3 million tonnes in 1997. A rather optimistic long-term forecast projects a 7-million-tonne figure by the year 2020 for all steel products including flat-rolled steel.

Perwaja has recently completed a 1.2-million-tonne DRI plant using HYL III technology. Its capacity is 600,000 tonnes a year. The plant cost $235 million. This plant uses a significant portion of the facilities, originally installed by Nippon Steel in 1985. Feed for the plant has been contracted for in the form of 1.5 million tonnes of pellets from several sources, including Chile, Sweden, and Bahrain. The pellets will be supplemented by 350,000 tonnes of lump ore from Brazil.

For steelmaking, Perwaja has contracted for two DC furnaces from NKK to increase its production from the current 1 million tonnes to 2.5 million by 1996. The group has proposed a rolling-mill division that would operate a mill producing

700,000 tonnes of structural sections. This will be installed in the near future.

The third group, Nusantara, does not operate a steelmaking facility. However, it plans to use the Mannesmann-Demag ISP technology which would have a capacity of 1.6 million tonnes of strip production. It would be installed at a cost of $960 million. Several Singapore and Hong Kong firms will take equity shares in the project; ownership will be 70 percent Malaysian and 30 percent foreign. The project will include two electric furnaces based on scrap. Part of the charge will be DRI. While it is unlikely that all three projects will materialize within the next few years, one or perhaps two will.

Malayawata Steel plans to install a DC furnace and a billet caster that will increase its raw steel capacity from 180,000 tonnes to 450,000 tonnes. The furnace and the caster will feed a rolling mill for rods that has been recently installed.

In 1993 steel capacity in Malaysia rose rapidly, according to the Malaysian Iron and Steel Federation. Steel demand is expected to grow by 10 percent in 1993, a much higher rate than that of previous years. The capacity for production rose to 3.5 million tonnes in 1993 from 2.0 million tonnes in 1992. A further increase in capacity of some 2.8 million tonnes has been approved for several projects due to be completed by 1995.

Indonesia. Indonesia has the benefit of Japanese investment in the production of galvanized sheets; Japanese investors include Nippon Steel, NKK, Mitsui, and Marubeni.

Indonesian steelmaking capacity will be further increased if two projects in the planning stage are eventually realized. Ispat plans to build a thin-slab minimill with a 1.2-million-tonne capacity. It also plans to expand its Krakatau works which has been in operation for some time. It will increase its capacity from 1.5 million tonnes to 2.5 million with an investment of some $480 million. A portion of this extra tonnage will be exported.

In a number of instances, one of these countries has engaged in a joint venture in another one. For example, an Indonesian group which brought an 800,000-tonne plate mill from Germany and installed it in Indonesia proposes to build a 2-million-tonne slab plant in Malaysia. It will be constructed and owned principally by the Gunawan Group.

In addition to these three countries, there is significant steel activity in two other countries, namely, Pakistan and Vietnam. In Pakistan, the state-owned steel works, based in Karachi, has undertaken an expansion program that will increase its output from somewhat less than 1 million tonnes to 2.8 million tonnes. This plan includes the installation of a third oxygen converter from Russia as well as an additional cold-rolling mill.

Pakistan Steel in connection with its expansion program is contemplating the installation of two Corex iron plants. These are C2000 Corex units, each of which would produce up to 700,000 to 800,000 tonnes a year. This would be a possible alternative to the installation of a blast furnace. Pakistan Steel is also negotiating for a used cold-reduction tandum mill with a 450,000-tonne capacity, in addition to a used tinning line for 200,000 tonnes. The company is interested in supplying the growing automobile industry in Pakistan.

In Vietnam, a rolling mill with a production capacity of 240,000 tonnes for bars and rods will be built at Ho Chi Minh City as a joint venture by the Japanese and the Vietnam Steel Union. It will be owned 40 percent by Vietnam and 60 percent by Mitsui; Ito Chu Corporation, formerly C. Itoh; and Kyoei Steel Works.

Some of the aforementioned projects may not materialize. However, most of them will, resulting in a substantial increase in capacity in Southeast Asia by the year 2000.

Argentina

The growth of the steel industry in Argentina during the past decade has been very slight. In 1982 production was 2.9 million tonnes, and in 1992 it was 2.7 million tonnes, having reached a high point of 3.9 million tonnes in 1989. The principal company, the government-owned Somisa, was recently privatized for an investment of $152 million, which was somewhat above the minimum of $140 million set by the government for the sale of 80 percent of the capital stock. The owners include an engineering group in Argentina, the Chilean steel group CAP, and Brazil's Usiminas and CVRD, the Brazilian iron ore company.

Since 1982 when exports were 789,000 tonnes, there has been a decided increase to a peak of 2,200,000 tonnes in 1989 with a subsequent decline in 1991 to 1,361,000 tonnes.

Mexico

Mexico privatized its steel industry in 1992. In connection with the privatization, the purchasers agreed to invest significant amounts of capital to improve the plants. AHMSA (Altos Hornos de Mexico) agreed to invest $500 million. Currently this program is in process. The principal item is the hot-strip mill which is being rebuilt at a cost of $200 million.

Venezuela

The Venezuelan steel industry consists of two companies, Sidor and Sivensa. Sivensa is privately held while Sidor is a public company. It is, however, in the process of privatization at the present time.

Middle East

The steel industry in the Middle East has grown considerably in the last two decades. In 1970, total production was 525,000 tonnes which consisted of an estimated 450,000 tonnes from Egypt, 60,000 from Israel and 15,000 from other countries. By 1980, production increased as a number of other countries began to produce steel. In that year, production was listed for Iran, Israel, Qatar and others. Total output was 1.9 million tonnes. By 1990, a number of other countries had begun steel production including Saudi Arabia, and production for the area increased to 4 million tones. In 1993, Egypt was classified under Africa and figures for the Middle East were given for Iran, Israel, Qatar, and Saudi Arabia, making a total of 6.8 million tonnes. If Egypt were classified with the Middle East, it would add 2.8 million tonnes more or a total of 9.6 million tonnes. Thus, growth over a 20-year-period has been significant.

As for the future, there are expansion plans in a number of countries including Egypt, which expects its steel consumption by 1997 to be in excess of 4 million tonnes. By the year 2002, Egypt projects some 5.4 million tonnes of consumption. Capacity by 1997 will be in the area of 3 million tonnes. Thus Egypt will be dependent on imports for a significant amount of its steel.

Saudi Arabia which was for many years dependent completely on imports, in 1982 totaling 5.3 million tonnes, has reduced its dependence considerably. In 1990, with its production of 1.8 million tonnes, imports were reduced to 1.6 million tonnes. The region has reduced its total dependence on imports from 14.1 million tonnes in 1982 to 10.2 million tonnes in 1991. Additional growth in the years ahead will result in a further decline of imports.

The area is also reducing its dependence on outside ore as is exemplified by the development in Iran of two major ore properties. One is the Bafq mine where output will be increased from 3 million to 5 million tonnes and the second is a mine at Sangan with a production of approximately 500,000 tonnes per year which is to be increased to 2 million tonnes.

The industry in the Middle East is serviced by electric-furnace operations as well as basic oxygen. Iran has 75 percent basic oxygen and 25 percent electric furnace, while Egypt has 40 percent basic oxygen, 54 percent electric and 6 percent open hearth. In terms of continuous casting, Saudi Arabia has 100 percent as does Qatar and Iran, while Egypt has 96 percent.

The Middle East is a growth area in terms of steel for the remainder of the current decade as well as in the beginning of the next century.

Conclusion

In analyzing the future plans for the industrialized countries as well as those for the developing countries, one finds that the attitude of the industrialized countries toward the future of their industries is one of realism somewhat tinged with pessimism. It manifests itself in the impression that the steel industry is, if anything, a limited growth industry for the remainder of the decade and into the first part of the twenty-first century. This attitude contrasts with the attitude of the developing countries toward their steel industries: the latter are more optimistic about the future as illustrated by their plans for growth and expansion.

These contrasting views stem from the fact that the industrialized countries have had a steel industry actively operating for a number of decades, and in some areas have reached a saturation point in terms of steel usage. This is particularly true in terms of construction and infrastructure. On the other hand, the developing countries have but recently entered the steel industry with major construction of facilities. They have a much larger growing market, particularly for such items as infrastructure. There is need in these countries to develop steel output in order to fulfill the basic requirements that were fulfilled long ago in the industrialized countries. The infrastructure in the industrialized countries will still require considerable steel, but mostly for replacement, whereas in the developing countries much of the infrastructure still remains to be built.

With the growth of the industry in the developing countries, they have become a smaller market for exports from the industrialized countries, particularly those in the EC and Japan. These exports have dwindled significantly since 1985. In that year, the EC countries shipped a total of 39 million tonnes outside their group plus 33 million tonnes within their group, for a total of 72 million tonnes. In 1991 total exports of the EC were 75.7 million tonnes, of which 50 million tonnes were exchanged within the community and 25.7 million shipped outside of it. Thus, in a period of six years, exports by the EC countries to destinations outside their own group dropped from 39 million tonnes to 25 million tonnes. The drop in EC exports was particularly notable in such areas as the USSR and Eastern Europe, when they fell from 7.9 million tonnes to 1.8 million tonnes. Likewise, EC exports to North America declined from 7.9 million tonnes to 4.8 million tonnes during the same period. Exports to Africa declined from 4.4 million tonnes to 2.5 million tonnes. The tonnage shipped to the People's Republic of China and North Korea fell from 4 million tonnes to 0.4 million.

The participation of the EC in trade outside its own sphere has declined considerably. This is due, in great part, to the growth in steel production in the developing countries as well the growth in exports by these countries to markets formerly serviced by the EC group. There is every indication that this export tonnage from the EC to noncommunity countries will continue to decline in the years between 1993 and 2000 due to the projected growth of production in the developing countries as well as their exports. As a consequence, it is felt that the EC will need less capacity in the years ahead with the reduction in its exports. The same will be true of Japan, whose exports fell from a high of 37 million tonnes in 1976 to 18 million tonnes in 1992.

The growth of steelmaking in the developing countries has been highly significant since 1980: their steel production doubled between 1980 and 1992. As previously indicated, there are plans to expand capacity considerably in the years ahead, particularly in the People's Republic of China, Taiwan, India, and the Republic of Korea. This expanded capacity will go into competition with the steel produced in the industrialized countries as the decade proceeds to the year 2000. The developing countries' share of the world's total steel production stands at 29 percent in 1993 and could well surpass 40 percent by the year 2000, with their export tonnage increasing to more than 40 million tonnes by that time. As a consequence, the industrialized countries' share of world production will diminish as the tonnage from the developing countries expands. This is the basic explanation why the industrialized countries have limited plans for expansion of steel capacity between 1993 and 2000. Their plans concern cost reduction and improved quality.

In the industrialized countries, no significant future growth in the domestic use of steel or its export is anticipated. On the other hand, the developing countries with their very large populations, such as 1.2 billion people in China and 800–900 million in India, will require more steel to improve their standard of living. Such items as construction, particularly infrastructure, and the development of an automobile industry will require additional tonnages by these countries as compared with the present time. The buildup in steel capacity in the developing countries, as well as the minor decline in capacity in the industrialized countries, will set the stage for more competition between the two areas.

3
Minimills versus Integrated Mills

T he minimill, a classic example of the way new technology drives competition, emerged some three decades ago as a means of exploiting continuous casting, then in the initial stages of its commercial introduction. The early minimills used simple continuous-casting machines for billets to link the electric steelmaking furnaces and flexible rolling mills common to their small-scale forerunners, and were able to enter the steel business on a highly competitive basis and for a very limited investment. Initially, they produced long, merchant products not requiring high-grade steel, including rebar, small channels, and angles, for sale within a geographic radius of a few hundred miles. But as continuous-casting technology advanced, so did the role of minimills. Increasing in number and size, their capability eventually extended to the entire long-products segment, which they now dominate in many countries around the world.

Once again, new continuous-casting technology is helping minimills acquire a commercial foothold in the steel business, this time in the flat-rolled market. New techniques to continuously cast "thin" slabs are reducing the large plant-scale and capital-cost requirements associated with conventional, "thick" slab casters and their downstream rolling and processing facilities. This is enabling minimills to increase their heretofore very limited sheet market participation. The question naturally arises as to whether the decades to come will see minimills make the same kind of headway in the flat-rolled business as they have in taking over the production and sale of many long-steel products.

This chapter examines the competitive challenges that minimills pose to traditional, integrated producers of flat-rolled steel. It does so from an historic, economic, and technical perspective. Because commercialization of the thin-slab minimill thus far has been a predominantly United States phenomenon, it focuses on the U.S. flat-rolled market, establishing the relationship between demand and supply as a means of gauging the likely future impact of new minimill competitors. Finally, the chapter reviews the worldwide status of projects aimed at installing thin-slab casters and discusses the outlook for new flat-rolled capacity in both the industrialized and the developing countries.

Steel Technology and the Minimill

The forerunners of today's minimills owed their beginnings to dramatic changes in electric-furnace steelmaking during the period immediately following World War II. Long used to produce small quantities of specialty alloy and stainless steel, the electric furnace underwent a number of technological improvements that transformed it into a scrap-melting producer of carbon steel. Furnace size was gradually increased, ultrahigh power was applied, and advances were made in furnace electrodes, electrode holders, refractories, and top-charging techniques. These innovations opened the door for small steel companies, permitting them to start steelmaking operations for a relatively small investment.

Electric-furnace steelmakers of the 1950s met with success in North America, Western Europe, and the Far East, concentrating on merchant steels and benefiting from their limited size and greater flexibility in a business otherwise dependent on large-scale operations. The small plants were particularly prominent in the United States, where companies such as Northwestern Steel and Wire, Laclede, Atlantic, Conners, and Knoxville Iron paved the way for many more to come. They also prospered in Italy's Padania area, in and around Brescia, a nineteenth-century charcoal-producing center, where the electric furnace was used to build a modern-day steel industry that has become widely known as the Bresciani.

As continuous casting began to be commercialized in the early 1960s, its initial success was in shaping billets, the semifinished shape most electric-furnace steelmakers rolled. Just as fortuitous, the limited capacity of early casting machines made them well suited to small plants, but inadequate to meet the semifinished needs of larger plants. This gave small, electric-furnace steelmakers a leg up on their large, integrated competitors in adopting a new technology that was to have a major impact in reducing production costs. It was soon recognized that continuous casting allowed small plants to produce efficiently certain kinds of steel without the scale economies that for so long had necessitated high-volume production. Thus the "minimill" phenomenon was born, a product of the turbulent 1960s.

Often forgotten because of the more recent growth and development of minimills around the world is just how *small* the early versions and their investment requirements were. In the mid-1960s the minimill approach made it possible to enter the steel business for less than $5 million to produce 50–60 thousand tons of long products annually. In 1966, for example, Tennessee Forging Steel Corporation started up a 60,000-ton minimill at Harriman, Tennessee. The plant's total investment cost was $4,200,200, with $2,760,000 going for land, building, and equipment, including an electric furnace, a twin-strand caster, a single-stand rougher, and a four-stand finishing mill. The company's product mix included forging quality billets, rebar, angles, and smooth rounds.

The early success of minimills in the United States and Italy prompted their spread to other parts of Europe, Canada, Japan, the Middle East, Latin America, and Southeast Asia. A catalyst behind their proliferation was the Korf Group, headed by German industrialist Willy Korf, who installed and operated mini-mills in Germany, France, the United States, and Brazil. In part reflecting the formation of new minimill companies, the world's production of electric-furnace steel rose from 38 million tonnes in 1960 to 87 million tonnes in 1970. This boosted the electric-furnace share of world crude steel output from 11.0 per-cent to 14.6 percent, at a time when overall world steel produc-tion was in a rapid growth phase, increasing by some 250 million tonnes.

Within a few years of their initial introduction, minimills were able to take advantage of high productivity and low costs to undersell integrated plants in most long-product markets. The ability to do so also derived from the low margins the integrat-eds traditionally realized on long products, which, during the 1970s, also weighed in decisions by many integrateds to grad-ually withdraw from long-product markets. In time, virtually all the merchant long products were left to the minimills, and there-after many integrateds, particularly in the United States and Ja-pan, also decided to abandon wire-rod production. Minimill product lines were extended to include wire, smooth rounds, special-quality flats, hexagons, joists, plates, ERW tubing, seamless tubing, special-bar quality (SBQ) bars, medium struc-turals, and eventually heavy structurals.

The Minimill Transformation

By the mid-1980s, as minimills moved toward domination in most long-product markets, they had proliferated around the world and had undergone dramatic increases in the size and complexity of their operations. By one count, there were 330 minimills worldwide as of 1984, including 132 in Western Eu-rope, 80 in Asia, 59 in North America, 40 in Latin America, 10 in Africa, 7 in the Middle East, and 2 in Oceania. Leading mini-mill countries included Italy, with 75; the United States, with 50; and Japan, with 25. Minimill capacity totaled 18.4 million tonnes in Western Europe, 17.8 million tonnes in Asia, and 16.7 million tonnes in North America.[6]

Minimill size, contrary to terminology and concept, had graduated upward, so that many minimills had capacities in excess of 300,000 annual tons, directed at producing more diverse and sophisticated product lines for distribution in widening geographic markets. Such was the incongruity of referring to some of these mills as "mini" that the steel lexicon expanded to embrace such terms as *midimills, maximills,* and *market-mills* in an effort to keep up with what the minimill of the 1960s had become.

As the number and size of minimills increased, so too did their problems. The harsh realities of world steel's pervasive hard times in the early- to mid-1980s saw many minimills struggling for survival just like their integrated counterparts. Some minimills went bankrupt, others failed and were permanently shut down, and many more underwent shifts in ownership and consolidation, demonstrating that the minimills were far from immune to the steel industry's problems.

By the time the minimill concept was about twenty years old, a growing number of the world's minimills no longer conformed to the formula so instrumental in their early success. They had developed in directions that found them confronting an increasingly difficult production and marketing environment. As their traditional product lines had matured, they had diversified the mix of steels they produced, and in a further effort to sustain their initial growth, they had scaled up their plant sizes beyond the requirements of their surrounding markets. Of necessity, they sought to distribute their increased output over much greater distances, eventually meeting severe competition, not only from integrated mills and imported steel, but from other minimills as well.

Faced with limited opportunities for added growth in long-product markets, minimills started to consider seriously the possibility of producing flat-rolled products. Although electric-furnace steelmaking had long been employed in producing plates and a limited variety of sheets and strip, most flat-rolled steels were widely regarded as beyond the technical capabilities of minimills, in significant part because of the scale requirements attached to conventional slab-casting and hot-strip-mill operations. However, this situation started to change once the near-net-shape casting of slabs moved toward commercialization, promising to open up sheet production to smaller scale plants characterized by reduced capital needs.

By 1986, Nucor was on the verge of installing its first "thin-slab" caster using technology developed by Schloemann-Siemag (SMS), and other minimills were also focusing on the flat-rolled business. Jeffry Werner, a senior vice-president of Chaparral, explained his company's interest as follows: "The whole [U.S. structural market is 6 million tons, mostly wide-flange beams, and we've determined that for every percent of market share you get, your price goes down one percent. . . We have saturated the bar and light-shapes market, what is left is flat-rolled, and the opportunity for growth in mini-mills truly does lie in flat-rolled."[7]

Minimills and Thin-Slab Casting

On a worldwide basis, there are now four minimills with thin-slab casters engaged in the commercial production of flat-rolled sheets, with combined annual capacities totaling 3.0 million tonnes. In the United States, two of the four plants are operated by Nucor: one at Crawfordsville, Indiana, with a hot-rolled capacity of 907,000 tonnes, and the other at Hickman, Arkansas, with a capacity of 1.1 million tonnes. At Cremona, Italy, a 500,000-tonne plant is operated by Arvedi, and at Avesta, Sweden, another 500,000-tonne plant, this one for stainless sheets, is run by Avesta Sheffield. The four plants utilize three different thin-slab technologies: SMS Concast casters are incorporated into the two Nucor installations, and Arvedi and Avesta use Mannesmann-Demag (MDH) and Voest-Alpine (VAI) technologies, respectively. These and other alternative approaches to casting thin slabs are described in chapter 5 on new steel technology.

In addition to the new flat-rolled producers with thin-slab casters, electric-furnace steelmakers with plants generally configured like minimills have long been active in producing steel plates and stainless sheets, while other minimills have installed facilities to produce sheets and strip using more conventional continuous-casting techniques. These thick-slab minimills include Tokyo Steel in Japan, with 1.0 million tonnes of capacity; Ipsco in Canada, with 800,000 tonnes; and NS Group in the United States, with 508,000 tons. The latter two producers use much of their output to support their own welded pipemaking operations.

Although minimills currently account for a minor 2 percent share of the approximately 350 million tonnes of hot-rolled coil capacity in place worldwide, their role in the flat-rolled business is bound to increase, given the number of thin-slab-casting projects now being pursued around the world. The list of projects in table 3–1 indicates the fourth-quarter, 1993, status of fifty-two existing and potential thin-slab casters in twenty-one countries, including sixteen in the United States, four each in Japan and South Korea, three each in Malaysia and China, two each in Belgium, Czechoslovakia, India, Russia, and Turkey, and single projects in Australia, Germany, Indonesia, Italy, Mexico, the Netherlands, Saudi Arabia, South Africa, Spain, Taiwan, and Venezuela.

Twenty of the fifty-two projects have progressed beyond active study, with four in operation, three under construction, four on order, and nine the subject of firm plans. These twenty projects would boost world thin-slab-casting capacity to 33 million tonnes, more than ten times its current level. It is, of course, most uncertain that all of this capacity will be installed, and it is even less likely that all of the thirty-two other projects still under study will be carried to completion. In fact, seven additional projects have already been studied and rejected. However, the extent of worldwide interest and activity suggests that a major expansion of thin-slab-casting capacity is likely to be made in the years ahead.

Because thin-slab casting permits flat-rolled production to be initiated in smaller than traditional increments, the adoption of this new technology can be expected to increase minimill participation in the flat-rolled business. The four thin-slab casters already in operation, two at Nucor's plants and one each at Arvedi and Avesta, are indicative of the technology's adaptability to minimill plant configurations and operating philosophies, despite involving capacities ranging from 500,000 to 2.0 million annual tonnes. However, it is likewise significant that the upper limits of their capacity range also make thin-slab casting adaptable to integrated steel plants.

Notably, a number of integrated steelmakers are currently pursuing thin-slab projects, including Hoogovens, Iscor, Posco, AHV, Dofasco, Geneva, Acme, Armco, and United States Steel, and although some of them plan to implement the technology by constructing their own stand-alone minimills, others, including Geneva and Acme, intend to incorporate this technology into their existing integrated plants, where the new casters are to be supplied with BOF steel.

The question of just who will install tomorrow's thin-slab casters is a most interesting one. In the 1960s new continuous-casting technology gave potential new steel producers an opportunity to enter the merchant steel business for less than $5 million. Today, new technology, namely, the thin-slab caster, is once again lowering the economic barriers to entry. Only this time around the investment ante is up to 70 times greater, or $350 million, which, even allowing for capital-cost inflation since the mid-1960s, places and funding requirement for entering the flat-rolled business beyond the reach of most minimill companies. Alternative casting and rolling technologies make it possible to attain a more limited participation in the business for a lower capital cost, although even in such cases an investment of $100–200 million is required. For this reason, it will probably become common for potential market entrants to seek joint-

Table 3–1
World Thin-Slab-Casting Capacity: Project Status
(millions of annual tonnes)

Country/Company/Location	Initial Capacity	Planned Additions	Status
Australia/Compact/E. Rockingham	1.7	—	Active study
Belgium/ALZ/Jenk	0.5	—	Studied, status unknown
Belgium/FAFER/Charleroi	0.7	—	Studied, status unknown
China/Pearl River-FALK/Zhujiang	0.8	—	Firm plans
China/Baoshan/Ningbo	1.5	1.5	Active study
China/Sougang/Beijing	1.0	—	Active study
Czechoslovakia/NHO/Kunice	—	—	Active study
Czechoslovakia/Trinec/Trinec	—	—	Active study
Germany/EKO/Eisenhuttenstadt	0.9	—	Firm plans
India/Kalinga/Daitari	3.0	—	Active study
India/Nippon-Denro Ispat/Alibagh	2.0	—	Active study
Indonesia/PT Ispat/Surabaya	1.2	—	Active study
Italy/Arvedi/Cremona	0.5	—	In operation
Japan/Kyoei/Soma City	—	—	Active study
Japan/Toa/Kashima	—	—	Active study
Japan/Tokyo/Yakkaichi	0.8	—	Active study
Japan/Yamato-Nucor/TBS	1.0	—	Studies, status unknown
Malaysia/Nusantara/Port Klang	1.6	—	Ordered
Malaysia/ASM Megasteel/Selangor	1.8	3.6	Firm plans
Malaysia/Perwaja/TBS	1.2	—	Active study
Mexico/Hylsa/Monterrey	0.7	0.8	Under construction
Netherlands/Hoogovens/IJmuiden	1.0	—	Active study
Russia/Amurstal/Komsomolsk	1.0	1.0	Active study
Russia/Novolipetsk/Lipetsk	1.0	—	Active study
Saudi Arabia/Saudi/Al-Jubail	—	—	Active study
South Africa/Iscor/Saldanha Bay	1.0	1.0	Studied, status unknown
South Korea/Hanbo/Asan Bay	1.0	0.7	Ordered
South Korea/Posco/Kwangyang Bay	1.0	—	Active study
South Korea/Dongbu/TBS	—	—	Studied, status unknown
South Korea/Dongkuk/TBS	—	—	Studied, status unknown
Sapin/AHV/Sestao	1.0	—	Firm plans
Sweden/Avesta Sheffield/Avesta	0.5	—	In operation
Taiwan/Yieh United/TBS	2.0	—	Ordered (on hold)
Turkey/Cuckurova/Izmir	1.5	—	Ordered (on hold)
Turkey/TDCI/Iskenderun	1.5	—	Studied, status unknown
USA/Nucor/Crawfordsville IN	0.9	0.8	In operation
USA/Nucor/Hickman AR	1.1	0.9	In operation
USA/Dofasco-CoSteel/Warsaw KY	0.9	1.4	Under construction
USA/Geneva/Vineyard UT	1.7	—	Under construction
USA/Acme/Riverdale IL	1.0	1.0	Firm plans
USA/Armco/Mansfield OH	0.7	0.3	Firm plans
USA/Birmingham/TBS	1.0	1.0	Firm plans
USA/Ipsco/Midwest TBS	1.0	—	Firm plans
USA/Nucor-Oregon/W. Coast TBS	1.0	1.0	Firm plans

Table 3–1 (Continued)
World Thin-Slab-Casting Capacity: Project Status
(millions of annual tonnes)

Country/Company/Location	Initial Capacity	Planned Additions	Status
USA/Beta/Portage IN	1.0	—	Active study
USA/California/Fontana CA	1.0	—	Active study
USA/Chaparral/TBS*	0.8	—	Active study
USA/North Star/TBS	1.0	—	Active study
USA/Steel Dynamics/Midwest TBS	0.9	0.9	Active study
USA/Tuscaloosa/Tuscaloosa AL	—	—	Active study
USA/USS-Worthington/Midwest TBS	1.8	—	Active study
Venezuela/Sidor TBS	—	—	Studied, status unknown

Source: John C. Groves, Metek Interstahl, unpublished database adapted by author.
*TBS as location designates plant site "to be selected."

venture partners as a means of sharing the cost, nor will it be unusual for minimills to team up with integrated mills, a development that has already started to emerge.

When Nucor initiated commercial thin-slab casting at Crawfordsville in 1989, the company expressed its intentions to participate only in the lower quality end of the flat-rolled business. This early market strategy reflected the limitations inherent in the technology at the outset of its commercial development and the additional limitations imposed by its use in a minimill-type configuration. Linked to scrap-based steelmaking, the caster was fed with steel prone to tramp-element contamination, and the resulting slabs, initially replete with surface and other quality problems, were rolled to a restricted range of widths and gauges. Over the past three to four years, however, considerable progress has been made in addressing technical problems at the caster, particularly those resulting in defective slab surfaces. Steel quality has been upgraded by using direct-reduced iron (DRI) to dilute contaminants in the scrap, and a fifth stand has been added to the hot mill to permit the rolling of thinner gauges.

With the refinements at Crawfordsville and the successful transfer of its knowhow to a second thin-slab unit at Hickman, Nucor has been considering a broader market strategy aimed at future participation in the higher quality sheet business. Toward this end, the company recently announced construction in Trinidad of the world's first commercial-scale plant to produce iron carbide, a clean-iron charge material to be used in upgrading the melt at Crawfordsville and Hickman. On May 14, 1993, at a minimill conference in Milan, Italy, Nucor's president, John Correnti, indicated that access to iron carbide would enable his company to produce sheets for automobile fenders and exposed appliance applications. Assuming iron carbide can be produced commercially, he had this to say about the prospects for Nucor's use of thin-slab casting: "In the future, we will see the evolution and refinement of this process such that the products will be sold very competitively in the high grade markets as well. The definition of high grade cold rolled strip would include class one products such as automobile fenders and exposed appliance applications. The time frame for this occurrence could be two to five years."[8]

Another U.S. minimill company, North Star, in announcing a joint-venture study with Australia's BHP on constructing a thin-slab caster and hot mill, stated that "the two companies aim to produce hot-rolled coil of higher quality than that currently made by Nucor. The proposed mill would focus on non-commodity grades like high carbon and low alloy."[9] Similarly, Arvedi in Italy has its sights set on adjusting the facilities and operations at its Cremona minimill to produce thinner gauge carbon sheets and stainless sheets; longer term, the company has given thought to a second minimill to produce between 1.5 and 2.0 million tonnes of low-carbon sheets for the automotive market.[10] In seeking participation in the flat-rolled business, therefore, minimills have started to target the market for sheets of higher quality than those produced by the pioneering Nucor plants in the early stages of their operation, and this strategy will eventually increase the competitive challenge that minimills pose for integrated flat-rolled producers.

As noted at the outset, the commercial use of thin-slab casting has been predominantly a U.S. phenomenon, a truth underscored by the list of active thin-slab projects in table 3–1, which shows that the United States has sixteen entries, four times more than any other country. Nucor entered the flat-rolled business some four years ago and currently has major expansions underway at both its Crawfordsville and Hickman thin-slab plants. Existing flat-rolled capacity at U.S. minimills, including thin-slab and conventional capacity, currently exceeds 4 million annual tonnes, and Nucor and CoSteel-Dofasco are installing another 2.6 million tonnes. In all, U.S. nonintegrated steelmakers with electric furnaces account for nearly 9 million tonnes of flat-rolled capacity, or 14 percent of the industry-wide total.

In the discussion to follow, the impact of new minimill competitors on the flat-rolled business is considered from a U.S. perspective, using the *net ton* designation to examine the current and future relationship between flat-rolled supply and demand.

U.S. Industry Environment

The massive size and awesome power that for so long led so many to believe that integrated steel plants were somehow immortal belied a vulnerability to economic and technical change that has dramatically recast the U.S. steelmaking environment since the mid-1970s. The long list of U.S. integrated plants that have met their demise certainly makes the long-term viability of some that remain a serious and particularly relevant issue. Evolving changes extending into the next century, including continued restructuring, heightened competition, and ongoing technological change, will continue to impact the industry environment, and in turn the future roles played by integrated mills and minimills, particularly as the latter seek to enter the flat-rolled business.

Over the past fifteen to twenty years, the U.S. steel industry has undergone the most drastic restructuring in the history of industrial enterprise. Confronted with declining demand, considerable excess capacity, and ultimately, ruinous financial

Table 3–2
U.S. Integrated Steel Plants in 1975 and Their Current Status

Plants	Status
1 Alan Wood/Conshohocken	X Shut down
2 Armco/Ashland	1 Linked to Middletown
3 Armco/Middletown	2 Operates as joint venture with Kawasaki
4 Armco/Houston[a]	X Shut down
5 Bethlehem/Bethlehem	3 Operating
6 Bethlehem/Burns Harbor	4 Operating
7 Bethlehem/Johnstown	X Shut down
8 Bethlehem/Lackawanna	X Shut down except for coke ovens
9 Bethlehem/Sparrows Point	5 Operating
10 CF&I/Pueblo	X Operates with electric furnaces
11 Crucible/Midland	X Operates with electrics and J&L Specialty Steel
12 Cyclops/Portsmouth	X Shut down
13 Ford/Rouge	6 Operates as Rouge Steel
14 Georgetown/Georgetown[b]	7 Operating
15 Indland/Indiana Harbor	8 Operating
16 Interlake/S. Chicago	9 Operating
17 J&L/Aliquippa	X Shut down
18 J&L/Cleveland	10 Operating as part of LTV/Cleveland
19 J&L/Pittsburgh	X Shut down except for coke ovens
20 Kaiser/Fontana	X Shut down except for finishing; now Cal. Steel
21 Lone Star/Lone Star	X Operates with electric furnaces
22 McLouth/Detroit	11 Operating
23 National/Granite City	12 Operating, principal owner NKK
24 National/Great Lakes	13 Operating, principal owner NKK
25 National/Weirton	14 Operating as Weirton Steel
26 Oregon/Portland[b]	X Operates with electric furnaces
27 Republic/Buffalo	X Shut down
28 Republic/Cleveland	—Operating as part of LTV/Cleveland, See No. 10
29 Republic/Gadsden	15 Operating as Gulf States
30 Republic/Massilon-Canton	X Operates with electrics as Republic Eng. Steels
31 Republic/S. Chicago	X Shut down except coke ovens
32 Republic/Warren	15 Operating as WCI Steel
33 Republic/Youngstown	X Shut down
34 Sharon/Sharon	X Shut down under Chapter 11
35 U.S. Steel/Edgar Thomson	17 Operating
36 U.S. Steel/Fairfield	18 Operating
37 U.S. Steel/Fairless	X Shut down
38 U.S. Steel/Gary	19 Operating
39 U.S. Steel/Geneva	20 Operating as Geneva Steel
40 U.S. Steel/Homestead	X Shut down
41 U.S. Steel/Lorain	21 Operating as USS/Kobe joint venture
42 U.S. Steel/Nat.-Duquesne	X Shut down
43 U.S. Steel/South	X Shut down
44 U.S. Steel/Youngstown	X Shut down
45 Wheel.-Pitt./Monessen	X Shut down
46 Wheel.-Pitt. Steubenville	22 Operating

Table 3–2 (Continued)
U.S. Integrated Steel Plants in 1975 and Their Current Status

Plants	Status
47 Wisconsin/S. Chicago	X Shut down
48 Youngstown S&T/Brier Hill	X Shut down
49 Youngstown S&T/Campbell	X Shut down
50 Youngstown S&T/Ind. Harbor	23 Operating as LTV/Ind. Harbor

Note: Youngstown Sheet & Tube was absorbed by J&L in December 1978; J&L and Republic then merged in 1984 to form LTV Steel, which sought protection under Chapter 11 of the bankruptcy laws in July 1986 and emerged from Chapter 11 in June 1993.

[a] Integrated via blast-furnace and direct-reduction routes.

[b] Integrated via direct reduction.

losses, steel companies have pursued radical rationalization programs and have made varied financial and operating changes that have restructured the industry from its very foundations. Mergers, buyouts, spin-offs, and joint ventures involving both domestic and foreign participants have all played a role in the restructuring process, and together with new minimill construction have spurred a host of new company formations that have thoroughly reconfigured the industry's corporate and geographic structure.

The impact of rationalization, which at one point cut 48 million tons or 30 percent from the industry's raw-steel-making capability, has fallen most heavily on the larger, integrated companies. As table 3–2, indicates, more than half of the integrated plants that refined steel from blast-furnace or direct-reduced iron in 1975 no longer do so. Their number fell from 50 to 23, even as the population of nonintegrated plants with scrap-based electric furnaces declined less than 7 percent from 108 to 100. Moreover, most integrated plants have been reduced in size, while many nonintegrated plants have continued to expand their capacities.

Thirteen of the plants where integrated steelmaking has been abandoned since 1975 once employed basic-oxygen (BOF) furnaces, ten had open hearths, and two used electric furnaces to refine direct-reduced iron (DRI). One final cut in the number of integrated plants, which did not result in an actual plant closure, came when LTV combined the former Cleveland operations of J&L and Republic. Notably, only four shutdowns of integrated steelmaking have occurred at plants with continuous casting, and five former integrated plants still conduct steelmaking operations, albeit on a smaller scale, by melting scrap in electric furnaces.

As a result of the restructuring process, a number of integrated producers gained their corporate independence from the major, multiplant companies, including Geneva Steel, Gulf States, USS/Kobe, WCI, and Weirton. Finally, Rouge Steel has been spun off by Ford Motor Company.

Restructuring Will Continue

As far-reaching as steel's restructuring has been, it is by no means over. The most obsolete and inefficient steel plants have already been closed, and the deepest cuts in capacity have already been made, so that future restructuring activity will have a less drastic impact on the industry environment. Nonetheless, steelmakers will continue to be confronted by financial, operating, and corporate changes for the extended future, in a restructuring that will include:

1. Some additional shutdowns of integrated plants and further rationalization of those that remain in order to streamline their product offerings.

2. Added shifts of output to the minimills and other nonintegrated producers.

3. Further increases in the industry's dependence on scrap-based operations.

4. Further geographic dispersion of the industry as additional production moves from the traditional steelmaking centers.

5. Additional changes in the industry's corporate composition through mergers, joint ventures, and other financial and op-

erating arrangements, involving both its integrated and non-integrated segments.

6. Added foreign participation in the industry, advancing the evolution of more of its member companies into internationalized enterprises.

The rate at which this future restructuring process occurs will be influenced by prevailing economic and steel-market conditions and their effects on the financial health of individual steel companies. Severe and protracted economic recessions that reduce steel demand and push down steel shipments for a year or more would hasten the further demise and rationalization of some integrated plants, and, depending on the drop in construction activity and the bar markets, could cause additional minimill casualties as well. As in the past, troubled times would act as a catalyst for mergers, acquisitions, joint ventures, and other financial arrangements promising a second life to otherwise failing companies and plants.

Significantly, poor times for the minimills would also slow their entry into upgraded steel markets by limiting their cash flows, profits, and access to the requisite investment capital. This was demonstrated a few years ago when Birmingham Steel dropped a planned $250-million venture to develop a minimill in Baytown, Texas, to produce up to 1.2 million tons of flat-rolled steel.

On the other side of the ledger, a strong steel market favoring sellers with higher prices and wider profit margins would slow restructuring activity and help keep existing plants in business. However, it would also provide increased incentives and improved conditions for investments in new and upgraded minimill capacity.

The state of the steel market, and so too the pace of future restructuring, will depend increasingly on global developments affecting the U.S. balance of trade in steel. Just as improved market conditions and higher domestic shipments in the late-1980s reflected the maintenance of competitive exchange values for the dollar and steady improvement in the steel-trade picture, the dollar's movement back to noncompetitive levels would eventually see market conditions deteriorate.

Relative exchange rates will also have a direct bearing on the role that foreign steel producers play in the future restructuring process. A lower dollar will make U.S. steel plants more attractive targets for foreign investment, while a higher dollar will make them less attractive. This is particularly true since a lower, more competitive dollar gives the United States preferred status as a base for all manufacturing operations, including those that produce and consume steel.

Competition Will Increase

The restructuring programs now in place acknowledge that the underlying trend in the steel business portends intense future competition for a market capable of modest growth in tonnage terms and comprised of consumers ever mindful and demanding of the utmost in product quality. The restructuring process has not only reconfigured corporate control over steel production, but together with an effective industry-wide modernization effort aimed at eliminating obsolete facilities and installing new technology, has also resulted in producing entities that are much more efficient and more able to compete, both at home and in overseas markets.

In effect, the old ways of doing business in steel, which left some room for marginal operations, are long gone. Today's market place is much less forgiving and points to a future industry environment that will be increasingly competitive in terms of quality, price, and customer service.

One of the most competitive segments of the steel market will be the flat-rolled product segment. It has been undergoing a quality revolution, as market demand has increasingly focued on sheets and strip rolled from "clean," continuously-cast steel to ever closer tolerances of uniform gauge and flatness, with critically applied coatings more and more in demand among automakers and other customers.

Two dozen domestic steel companies and a host of foreign steel producers vie for this business, and as the discussion to follow indicates, their combined supply capabilities are more than adequate to meet the market's flat-rolled requirements. This situation assures intense competition on a long-term basis and means that new market entrants, principally minimills using thin-slab technology, will have to acquire market share at the expense of existing domestic producers or imports, mainly by selling at below-market prices. Nucor found this strategy necessary when initiating sales of its commercial-grade coil. The future extent of such discounting will depend on the number of new minimill entrants and the market conditions they encounter in starting to sell their output.

Concerning the future competitive struggle between integrated steelmakers and minimills for the sheet business, it must be recognized that the facilities operated by the integrated companies are largely written off and that light, flat-rolled products represent the heart of their business. In the past, minimills have been able to take over noncore markets for reinforcing bar, structurals, and other long products that in some cases had become more or less expendable in the drive by integrated mills to rationalize their operations. By contrast, light, flat-rolled products account for a major share of integrated-mill output, and future attempts by newcommers to penetrate this market will be met with strong resistance.

An additional, important aspect of the future competitive environment that flat-rolled producers will have to face is the ongoing development and promotion of substitute materials, which are bound to make additional inroads into traditional steel markets as their cost and performance characteristics improve over time. Although steelmakers have thus far combined enhancements in sheet quality with competitive pricing and co-operative design and applications' work to slow the use of plastics and aluminum by automakers and other manufacturers, it would be unrealistic to conclude that the competitive threat from substitutes had been laid to rest.

As new technologies have started to lower the barriers to market entry, minimills seeking new growth outlets have initiated their market incursion by installing recently developed thin-slab casters directly linked to hot-strip rolling mills. In the future, as minimills install additional flat-rolled capacity and thin-slab casting progresses beyond initial commercialization and is eventually joined by strip-casting technology, the state-of-the-art in producing flat-rolled steel will be dramatically revolutionized. With new technology providing the catalyst, a protracted and intense competitive struggle will occur for a growing portion of what has long been a market segment almost totally dominated by integrated steel companies.

Trends in U.S. Steel Demand

The future competitive impact of minimills entering the flat-rolled market can best be considered within the context of expected conditions in the U.S. steel market in general. Although future demand requirements will have the potential to sustain, if not slightly increase, the business of flat-rolled producers on a long-term basis, the fact remains that their's is not a growth industry, and more than slight demand increases will be needed to absorb the output likely to be placed on the market by new minimill competitors.

Past Trends

During most of the last twenty years many factors external to the steel industry acted in concert to create a market for its products characterized by severe cyclical swings and troubling secular decline. The oil-price shocks of the 1970s, recurring shifts in international monetary relationships, and restrained economic growth all played a part, while still other factors, both external and internal to the industry, more directly and permanently impacted steel demand. These other factors were as follow:

1. The U.S. economy became more service-oriented, as increasing quantities of manufactured goods were obtained from overseas.

2. The focus of capital spending, usually the prime mover of the steel market, shifted away from heavy equipment and the construction of new plants toward the installation of computer systems, which consume very little steel.

3. With the nation's infrastructure largely in place, the government continued to neglect spending on public works in favor of funding extensive social programs.

4. In the key automobile industry, materials substitution and the downsizing of vehicles in the interest of fuel economy reduced the steel content of the average U.S. passenger car by 25 percent and cost the steel industry 10 million annual tons of consumption.

5. Substitute materials such as aluminum, glass, ceramics, plastics, and concrete moved into once-exclusive steel markets.

6. The steel industry itself contributed to the decline by introducing lighter-weight steels that perform the same functions as their heavier counterparts.

7. Steel consumers increased their steel-using efficiency by introducing computer-aided design (CAD) and manufacturing (CAM) techniques, therby increasing their production yields and reducing their steel needs per unit of output.

The combined result of these factors has been a secular trend of lower steel input in relation to the U.S. economy's overall domestic output. But since the mid-1980s this secular trend has become much more moderate, and steel demand has become more stable at significantly higher levels, all of which are encouraging developments for the steel-market outlook for the next twenty years.

Future Trends

Although the steel cycle is alive and well, there have been indications that the longer term trend of demand has been improving and that a somewhat more favorable relationship between steel use and economic activity is in the process of being reestablished. This is a long-term positive for the steel market, because it indicates that many of the demand restraints enumerated above are well along in their evolutionary development. In fact, much of their potential impact will have been realized in the near-term future. Consider the following:

1. The U.S. manufacturing sector has been undergoing a revival, due in part to a competitive exchange value for the dollar.
2. With an improved manufacturing climate, capital spending for new plants has also improved: witness the ongoing construction of new auto plants by foreign carmakers.
3. More attention is being paid to public works and infrastructure renewal, not because government has chosen to do so, but because more bridges have started to collapse.
4. American automobiles are once again getting larger.
5. Aluminum already has 96 percent of the beverage-can market.
6. The steel industry can ring only so much weight out of its products.
7. Computer-based yield savings in manufacturing are becoming harder to achieve, given an installed base of computer systems that is already widespread.

Clearly, the factors for decline in the economy's specific steel needs are running out of steam, and this portends a steel market capable of increasing on a trend basis, albeit at a very modest rate, as the economy expands into and beyond the current decade.

Although more favorable market conditions have already

started to emerge, there has been understandable reason for viewing the improved performance turned in by steelmakers in the late 1980s with a certain degree of caution. Steel production and shipments moved above trend in mid- to late-1987, and in that sense 1988–89 could be considered a boom period, particularly when viewed from the perspective of the severely depressed market a few years earlier and the cyclical decline that followed in 1991. However, a lot positive has happened to the industry since the dark days of 1982; moreover, since early 1985 the dollar has fallen substantially to much more competitive levels, acting in favor of U.S. manufacturing activity and steel demand.

The ongoing revival of the manufacturing sector underscores the fundamental changes that have taken place in steel's production and marketing outlook. On the production side, the industry, through its own effort, has become one of the most efficient in the world—and aided by the lower dollar, it has also become one of the most competitive. Since 1982, with nearly $25 billion pumped into new facilities, productivity gains have cut the industry's labor input per ton of shipments to less than half of what it was, and further improvement will result from the modernization programs presently underway. Meanwhile, the industry's customer base has also become more competitive and more capable of participating in a broader, international market.

A key contributor to internationalizing the industry's customer base has been the influx of overseas investment capital into the manufacturing sector to construct so-called transplants. In the auto industry alone, more than five hundred Japanese and European assembly and parts plants have been established, and before long about one-fifth of all Japanese auto-manufacturing capacity is likely to be located here, some of it targeted at the export market.

The fundamental changes in the steel industry and its market have positive implications for its prospects over the rest of the decade and beyond. The steel cycle, not as closely tied to the U.S. economy is likely to be more moderate on the downside than in the past, and the industry, given its improved cost structure and its own potential as an exporter, is now more able to contend with any downturn in the domestic steel market that does occur.

In the years ahead increases in the dollar's value will accompany definitive signs of a shrinking trade deficit. But the dollar will remain at levels that keep the steel industry competitive—and also keep the recently established transplants competitive. Their presence in the United States represents an insurance policy that Japanese and European influence in the international currency markets will help keep the dollar competitive into the long-term future. Meanwhile, it remains for steelmakers themselves to preserve and build upon the hard-fought and painful gains already made in order to solidify their long-term competitive position.

Looking to the future, there is, of course, a certain inevitability to steel imports into the U.S. market, given the industry's growing internationalization and the ever-more-complex patterns of trade in which steel is shipped across national boundaries. However, while imports are here to stay, this does not necessarily mean that they will inevitably rise to claim a larger segment of the market.

Together with the stronger competitive position now enjoyed by U.S. steelmakers, the long-term outlook for imports is being positively affected by the building overseas trend of steel privatization that will see a growing share of world steel capacity shifted from public to private ownership. Accordingly, more of the steel introduced into international trade in future years will be produced by profit-driven as opposed to subsidized companies, therby mitigating the predatory price competition that has been so destructive in the past.

Steel-Market Outlook through 2010

The steel-market forecast in table 3–3 recognizes the improved, long-term market conditions just described and conservatively provides for their future positive influence by assuming a dimin-

Table 3–3
U.S. Steel-Market Forecast through 2010
(millions of tons)

	Avg. 1988–92	1995	2000	2005	2010
GDP (bil. $ 1987)	$4,836	$5,380	$6,167	$6,949	$7,716
Steel per mil. $ GNP (tons)	19.9	18.5	16.5	15.0	14.0
Steel Demand	96.2	99.5	101.8	104.2	108.0
Imports	17.7	15.5	16.0	16.5	18.0
Exports	4.3	5.0	5.0	5.0	5.0
Steel Shipments	82.8	89.0	90.8	92.7	95.0

ished trend of decline in the specific steel input needed to support the U.S. economy's output. Although the previously enumerated restraints on steel demand will diminish, they will continue to impact the future steel market, particularly if substitute materials make additional market inroads.

Also assumed in the table 3–3 forecast is a slow-growth economy that averages a real annual GDP growth rate of 2.5 percent, down from the 3–4 percent historical norm. This future growth is projected to occur at a decelerating rate, from an average of 3.0 percent annually through 1995, down to 2.0 percent in 2010. Imports, including finished and semifinished products, are assumed to represent 15–16 percent of apparent consumption annually over the period, while exports are held constant at 5.0 million annual tons.

The forecast market tonnages represent trend values consistent with average levels of economic and steel industry activity and do not account for fluctuations about trend, either cyclical or random, that cannot be predicted as to timing or intensity over the long term. Divergencies from trend that may result from such causes as severe economic instability, additional oil-price shocks, or major product breakthroughs enhancing steel or its various substitutes are not reflected in the predicted values.

The table 3–3 forecast calls for levels of shipments approximating 90 million tons in 1995 and 2000, 93 million tons in 2005, and 95 million tons in 2010. All of these *trend* values compare favorably to the *peak* shipping volumes of 83–84 million tons realized during 1988–89 and indicate that, even with a slow-growth economy and additional market penetration by substitute materials, steelmakers should operate at better than a 90-million-ton shipments level during much of the period through 2010.

Flat-Rolled Demand through 2010

Turning to the outlook for the flat-rolled steel market, which is particularly pertinent to the developing competitive struggle between integrated mills and minimills, it is forecast to pursue a long-term trend roughly parallel to that projected for the total steel-product market.

For purposes of discussion here, *flat-rolled steel* is defined as those finished steel-mill products that are first processed beyond the semifinished stage using hot-strip mills. As such, flat-rolled steel is considered to include all products categorized in the American Iron and Steel Institute's (AISI) statistical reports as sheets and strip, tin-mill products, and plates in coils; and it also includes portions of the AISI product categories for cut-length plates and tubular products. One-fifth of all cut-length plates are rolled on hot-strip mills, as is skelp for in-house conversion into some 40 percent of all welded pipe and tube.

During the period 1988 to 1992, as table 3–4 indicates, flat-rolled market demand, measured in terms of apparent consumption (domestic shipments plus imports minus exports), averaged 54.4 million net tons, ranging from a low of 49.9 million tons in the recession year, 1991, to a high of 56.8 million tons at the peak of the steel cycle in 1988.

Table 3–4
U.S. Flat-Rolled Steel Market in 1988–92
(thousands of net tons)

	1992	1991	1990	1989	1988	Avg.
Shipments	48,528	45,420	48,963	49,831	49,251	48,399
Imports	9,449	8,022	8,594	7,953	9,030	8,610
Exports	2,206	3,592	2,304	3,254	1,468	2,565
Demand	55,771	49,850	55,253	54,530	56,813	54,444

Tables 3–5 and 3–6 set forth domestic flat-rolled shipments and the market's foreign trade components, respectively, and were compiled from AISI data, with calculations made for sheets and strip used in producing captive tubulars and for cut-length plates from hot-strip mills. Flat-rolled shipments during the years 1988–92 averaged 48.4 million tons, with imports and exports averaging 8.6 million and 2.6 million tons, respectively.

The 1992 flat-rolled market displays some significant differences from that of 1985, when the U.S. dollar was just beginning its long-term decline and U.S. steelmakers were in the early stages of extensive modernization programs. Much of their capital spending was to go into new galvanizing lines in response to the demands of auto, appliance, and other manufacturers. A comparison of the 1985 and 1992 flat-rolled markets reveals the ensuing changes in demand favoring galvanized sheet products. As table 3–7 indicates, the galvanized segment of the market expanded by nearly one-fourth, even as the aggregate demand for other flat-rolled products remained virtually the same. No-

Table 3–5
U.S. Shipments of Flat-Rolled Steel, All Grades, 1985 and 1988–92
(thousands of net tons)

	1992	1991	1990	1989	1988	1985
Sheet and Strip:						
Hot-rolled	13,911	13,694	14,080	13,983	13,792	13,538
Cold-rolled	13,524	12,287	14,015	14,724	14,812	14,450
Hot-dipped galv.	8,199	6,910	7,878	8,543	8,115	6,850
Electrolytic galv.	2,390	2,099	2,066	2,151	2,134	697
All other metallic coated	1,348	1,146	1,259	1,259	1,262	1,122
Electrical	436	458	486	484	524	413
For in-house tubulars[a]	1,181	1,263	1,309	1,129	1,250	1,153
Tin-mill products	3,927	4,041	4,031	4,126	4,069	3,773
Strip-Mill plates:						
Cut lengths[a]	872	855	1,026	1,017	1,009	865
In coils	2,740	2,667	2,813	2,297	2,284	[b]
Totals	48,528	45,420	48,963	49,831	49,251	42,861

Source: American Iron and Steel Institute, *Annual Statistical Report, 1992,* p. 26, 1989, pp. 24–25. Shipments are net of those reporting companies; Flat-rolled steel is that processed on hot-strip mills.

[a] Calculated by author.

[b] In sheets, hot-rolled.

Table 3–6
U.S. Imports of Flat-Rolled Steel, All Grades, 1985 and 1988–92
(thousands of net tons)

	1992	1991	1990	1989	1988	1985
Imports						
Sheets and Strip:						
Hot-rolled	2,812	2,226	2,378	2,009	2,256	2,848
Cold-rolled	2,299	2,029	2,188	2,017	2,240	2,967
Hot-dipped galv.	1,727	1,273	1,263	1,297	1,949	2,465
Electrolytic galv.	319	247	386	328	—	2,465
All other metallic coated	284	190	192	236	248	204
Electrical	82	82	76	85	74	118
For in-house tubulars[a]	434	770	731	696	924	1,256
Tin-mill products	606	555	574	597	546	786
Strip-Mill plates:						
Cut lengths[a]	181	160	192	188	235	276
In coils	705	490	614	500	558	[b]
Totals	9,449	8,022	8,594	7,953	9,030	10,920
Exports						
Sheets and Strip:						
Hot-rolled	479	1,671	757	1,201	451	69
Cold-rolled	467	518	476	587	116	56
Hot-dipped galv.	161	180	199	333	267	29
Electrolytic galv.	137	124	87	111	—	29
All other metallic coated	124	100	104	103	66	43
Electrical	48	84	48	55	43	14
For in-house tubulars[a]	191	212	132	125	70	56
Tin-mill products	344	194	176	218	431	164
Strip-mill plates:						
Cut lengths	39	55	34	27	24	17
In coils	216	454	291	494	—	[b]
Totals	2,206	3,592	2,304	3,254	1,468	448

Source: American Iron and Steel Institute, *Annual Statistical Report,* 1992, pp. 40, and 50; 1989, pp. 34–35, 44–45.
[a] Calculated by author.
[b] In sheets, hot-rolled.

tably, the market comparison also reflects the improved international competitive position of U.S. flat-rolled producers.

As to the future of the U.S. flat-rolled market, the forecast presented in table 3–8 projects trend values through 2010 consistent with the previously discussed outlook for the U.S. steel market in general. The increase in flat-rolled demand to 61.0 million annual tons over the period implies an extremely modest growth rate of 0.5 percent per annum from the 1988–92 aver-

Table 3–7
U.S. Flat-Rolled Steel Market in 1985 vs. 1992
(thousands of net tons)

	1985	1992	% Change
Shipments	42,861	48,528	13.2
Imports	10,920	9,449	-13.5
Exports	448	2,206	392.4
Demand	53,333	55,771	4.6
Galvanized	9,983	12,337	23.6
All other coated[a]	5,678	5,697	0.3
Uncoated	37,672	37,737	0.1

[a] Includes tin-mill products and all other metallic coated sheets and strip.

age demand level of 54.4 million tons. Allowing a future market share for imports in the 15–16 percent range and yearly exports averaging 3.0 million tons, domestic shipments are projected to move above the 50-million-ton level in 1995 and to reach 54.5 million tons on a trend basis in 2010.

Flat-Rolled Demand versus Supply

The degree of competitive resistance likely to be encountered by new minimill entrants into the flat-rolled business will depend to a great extent on just how demand stacks up against the industry's flat-rolled supply capability. Considering that all of the flat-rolled products included in the demand analysis above are first rolled on hot-strip mills, the addition to demand of an allowance for yield losses beyond the hot-rolling stage makes it possible to compare the market's current and future requirements for hot-strip-mill production and the hot-strip-mill ca-

Table 3–8
U.S. Flat-Rolled Steel Market through 2010
(millions of net tons)

	Avg. 1988–92	1995	2000	2005	2010
Shipments	48.4	50.7	51.5	53.0	54.5
Imports	8.6	9.0	9.0	9.0	9.5
Exports	2.6	3.0	3.0	3.0	3.0
Demand	54.4	56.7	57.5	59.0	61.0

pacity presently in place. The conclusion thereby reached is that capacity already in place is significantly in excess of current needs and is more than adequate to accommodate the extremely modest market growth anticipated over the next fifteen or more years. This means that new minimills will have to acquire market share either at the expense of existing producers or by displacing imports, which portends extremely competitive market conditions well into the next century.

The flat-rolled market forecast in table 3–8 can be expressed in terms of hot-strip-mill production by providing for an 8 percent average yield loss in downstream processing. Hot-rolled coils from the hot-strip mill are shipped as is, or are put through one or more additional processing steps to obtain a full range of flat-rolled products. Yield losses occur as coils are pickled and oiled, cold rolled, annealed, temper or skin rolled, and coated by tinning, by galvanizing, or by applying a variety of other finishes. The number of such processing steps varies from mill to mill, and so too the downstream yield losses each mill incurs vary. However, based on the experience of a cross section of mills, comparing their hot-rolled output and finished-product shipments, an 8 percent average yield loss represents a suitable proxy for the total mill population.

Accounting for this yield loss, U.S. flat-rolled shipments averaging 48.4 million tons annually during 1988–92 equated with a hot-strip-mill production requirement of 52.3 million tons. This average yearly volume of hot coils rolled on domestic mills, which went to support both domestic flat-rolled shipments and exports, will increase to a trend level of 58.9 million tons in 2010.

This trend output requirement does not allow for likely future improvements in downstream yields, and to this extent may be overstated. However, it is well within the aggregate production capabilities of U.S. hot-strip mills already in place, which, as the analysis to follow indicates, can turn out 67.6 million annual tons. This means there is enough current capacity to support not only domestic flat-rolled shipments, but also total market demand over the period through 2010.

How much steel can hot-strip mills roll? As much as can be run through them in a given period of time. But throughput is often limited by the market's needs, which go to make up order books and rolling schedules that call for varying sheet specifications. If, for example, the market requires mill-edged sheets narrower than a mill's maximum width capabilities, throughput will be less than optimal when these sheets are rolled. Likewise, limitatons at the melting and continuous-casting facilities to which the mill is linked can restrict the supply of slabs for rolling, although such shortfalls often can be made up, at least partially, by slab purchases, which notably have tripled industry-wide over the last ten years.

The hot-strip-mill capacities indicated in table 3–9 account for the limitations currently imposed on mill throughput by order-book composition and operating restrictions, including those imposed by the physical condition of the mills themselves, or by the capabilities of their support facilities from ironmaking through steelmaking, continuous casting or primary rolling, and finally slab reheating. The capacities also reflect the use of purchased slabs to augment internal slab supplies. As such, the capacity data presented, which were compiled in consultation with each of the listed companies, represent the real-world supply capabilities of their mills, accounting for their product-mix and facility limitations and assuming full-out operations.

In all, thirty-five hot-strip mills are operated by twenty-four steel companies at thirty-two plants situated in thirteen states; these mills have a combined effective rolling capacity of 67.6 million annual net tons. The greatest geographic concentration of mills is in the traditional steel-producing states in and around the Midwest and Great Lakes regions. There are seven mills in Indiana, six in Ohio, five in Pennsylvania, four in Illinois, three each in Alabama and Michigan, and one each in Arkansas, California, Kentucky, Maryland, Texas, Utah, and West Virginia. Three plants operate two mills, namely Acme/Chicago, LTV/Cleveland, and Inland/East Chicago.

Table 3–9
U.S. Hot-Strip Mills: Size, Type, and Capacities
(thousands of annual net tons)

Company & Plant[a]	Width (In.)	Type[b]	No. Stands[c] Rgh.	Fin.	Capacity
I Acme/Chicago IL	30	SC	1	6	775
I Acme/Chicago IL	10	C	5	5	35
N Al.Lud./Brackenbridge PA	56	SC	1	6	500
N Armco/Butler PA	58	SC	1	5	900
N Armco/Mansfield OH	52	SC	2	6	825
I Armco/Middletown OH(2)	86	C	6	7	4,020
N Beta/Portage IN	60	SC	1	5	800
I Beth./Burns Harbor IN(2)	80	C	5	7	4,100
I Beth./Sparrows Pt. MD	68	SC	2	6	2,900
N Calif./Fontana CA	86	C	4	6	1,500
I Geneva/Provo UT	132	SC	1	6	1,900
I Gulf States/Gadsden AL	54	SC	1	6	1,120
I Inland/E. Chicago IN (2)	80	C	6	6	4,500
I Inland/E. Chicago IN	76	C	5	6	400
N J&L/Midland PA	56	SC	1	5	425
I LTV/Cleveland OH (2)	84	C	5	7	2,100
I LTV/Cleveland OH (2)	80	SC	3	6	3,800
I LTV/Indiana Harbor IN (2)	84	C	6	7	4,100
N Laclede/Alton IL	22	C	5	5	250
N Lone Star/Lone Star TX	73	R	—	1	800
I McLouth/Trenton MI	60	SC	2	6	1,200
N NS Group/Wilder KY	50	R	1	2	560
I Nat./Ecorse MI (2)	80	C	5	7	3,400
I Nat./Granite City IL (2)	80	C	4	7	2,400
N Nucor/Crawfordsville IN	53	C	0	5	1,000
N Nucor/Hickman AR	61	C	0	6	1,200
I Rouge/Dearborn MI (2)	68	C	4	7	2,800
N Tuscaloosa/Tusca. AL	112	R	—	1	650
I USS/Fairfield AL	68	SC	1	6	1,800
I USS/Gary IN (2)	84	C	6	7	5,700
I USS/Irvin PA	80	C	5	6	2,850
I WCI/Warren OH (2)	56	SC	1	6	1,500
N Washington/Wash. PA	56	R	1	1	225
I Weirton/Weirton WV	54	SC	2	7	3,800
I Wheel.Pitts/Steub. OH (2)	80	C	4	6	2,800

Note: Capacities represent real, effective production capabilities at full operations and provide for melting, casting, and product-mix limitations, as well as for supplemental slab purchases.

[a] I = Integrated plant. N = Nonintegrated plant; (2) Indicates "second-generation" mill.

[b] C = Continuous; SC = Semi-Continuous; R = Reversing.

[c] Indicates number of roughing and finishing stands.

Integrated steel plants with blast furnaces and oxygen steel-making house twenty-two of the thirty-five mills and account for 58.0 million tons, or 86 percent, of the rolling capacity presently in place. Table 3–10 indicates the distribution of this integrated capacity by company.

Nonintegrated steel plants account for the thirteen remaining mills with 9.6 million tons of capacity or 14 percent of the total. Ten of the nonintegrated plants employ electric-furnace steelmaking, while three operate without steelmaking support and depend instead on outside sources of semifinished slabs, namely, Beta, California, and Tuscaloosa. Four nonintegrated plants roll stainless and other specialty steel products, namely, Allegheny-Ludlum, Armco/Butler, J&L, and Washington. Table 3–11 indicates nonintegrated capacity distributed by company.

Electric-furnace steelmaking is also used in sheet production within four integrated plants, namely, LTV/Cleveland, McLouth, National/Ecorse, and Rouge/Dearborn, which have a combined electric-furnace capacity of 1.7 million annual tons. This capacity is most often employed intermittently to supplement output from the BOF steelmaking shops that provide most of the steel requirement at each of these plants.

Among the thirty-five hot-strip mills presently operating, twelve were installed in the 1960s and early 1970s and were appropriately named "second-generation" mills because of the advances they afforded in rolling speed, closer strip tolerances, and larger coil sizes. Combined with the recently installed Nu-

Table 3–10
Hot-Strip Capacity of U.S. Integrated Mills

USS	10.35[*]	Rouge	2.80
LTV	10.00	Wheel.Pitt.	2.80
Bethlehem	7.00	Geneva	1.90
National	5.80	WCI	1.50
Inland	4.90	McLouth	1.20
Armco	4.02	Gulf States	1.12
Weirton	3.80	Acme	0.81

[*] Millions of net tons.

Table 3–11
Hot-Strip Capacity of U.S. Nonintegrated Mills, Distributed by
Companies

Nucor	2.20[a]	NS Group	0.50
Armco	1.73	Allegheny-Ludlum	0.50
California	1.50	J&L	0.43
Beta	0.80	Laclede	0.25
Lone Star	0.80	Washington	0.23
Tuscaloosa	0.65		

[a] Millions of net tons

cor mills, they are capable of rolling 41.2 million annual tons. The industry's twenty-one other mills were built mainly before World War II, or in the postwar years through the 1950s and have effective capabilities totaling an additional 26.4 million tons. Many of these mills have been extensively rebuilt and upgraded over the years to approach second-generation status, and in the last five years much of the total mill population has received considerable investment capital to bring their performance in line with advancing sheet-quality standards.

In order to meet customer demands, cut costs, and improve sheet quality, hot-strip-mill operations have had a clear-cut drive underway to roll as much of their output as possible from continuously-cast slabs. Limiting this trend, the continuous-casting capabilities of some plants are inadequate to support full-out rolling operations, and if they rolled only self-produced continuously-cast slabs, some 4.5 million tons would be pared from the industry's annual rolling capacity. However, to compensate for this potential caster constraint, strip-mill operators have been purchasing slabs from domestic and overseas suppliers, and rolling capacity in excess of 1.5 million tons continues to rely on slabs rolled from ingot-cast steel.

Segments of the Flat-Rolled Market

Competition between and among the industry's hot-strip mills depends upon each unit's product capabilities, determined, in turn, by the technical advances in rolling each embodies, the quality of its upstream steel supply through slabs for rolling, and the extent and sophistication of its downstream processing and coating facilities. The mills can be categorized according to their capabilities and the broad segments of the flat-rolled market in which they most often participate.

High-End

Second-generation and other extensively upgraded mills within integrated steel plants convert slabs to meet a full range of flat-product requirements across the market spectrum. The blast-furnace iron such plants produce is refined into clean steel low in residual-alloy contaminants, which is then continuously cast, rolled, and extensively processed into a diverse line of coated and uncoated sheet products.

Hot-strip mills in this top category are fully computerized and incorporate such advances as roll bending, side shifting, or pair-crossed rolling. They produce sheets of impeccable surface and with exacting mechanical properties to extremely close tolerances of gauge and flatness, including the deep-drawing grades that shape auto-body exteriors, the tinplate grades, and other high-quality sheets, both coated and uncoated, that command significant market premiums. But they also roll sheets for less-demanding applications, both on a scheduled basis and as secondary steels not meeting high-end standards, which brings them into competition with their midrange and low-end counterparts.

Midrange

Hot-strip mills in this midrange category primarily consist of those within smaller integrated plants that also refine blast-furnace iron and continuously cast their slabs. However, they have rolling and other operating limitations that preclude their consistently meeting the stringent quality standards required of high-end producers. Midrange mills also roll steel for processing into a broad line of coated and uncoated sheet products, but generally for less critical applications. Still, their capabilities in terms of width, gauge, surface quality, coating, and other downstream processing exceed those of their low-end competitors, including the new minimills with thin-slab casters.

Low-End

Mills with limited capabilities either in rolling or in their related steelmaking or downstream processing operations rank in this low-end category. They generally rely on melting scrap in electric furnaces and even if they purchase the best available scrap, it contains residual alloys in amounts that exceed the upper limits specified for most high-quality sheet products. This drawback can be overcome by adding direct-reduced iron or some other diluent to the furnace charge, although steelmaking and overall production costs are thereby increased. Relative to their higher ranked competitors, low-end mills also roll a more limited range of widths and gauges, generally to wider tolerances of both gauge and flatness, and they are linked to fewer, if any, downstream facilities. The flat products they market are often referred to as commodity-grade or commercial-grade steel and are puchased mainly for applications in which quality is less important than price.

Minimill sheet producers, which are in the early stages of their commercial development, presently rank as low-end market participants. Given the extent to which their technology, centered around their thin-slab casting, has so far evolved, minimills can supply only a limited range of sheet products. Higher quality sheets are beyond their current capability because of their dependence on scrap-based steelmaking, surface problems from the entrapment of casting-mild powders, width and gauge limitations at their rolling mills, and a paucity of coating and other downstream facilities.

In the future, minimills will achieve steel-quality and surface improvements by including virgin iron units in their electric-furnace charges and by redesigning the molds on their thin-slab casters. However, it is unlikely that they will develop the inclination or the funding capability to install downstream processing facilities as diverse and sophisticated as those presently operated by their larger, integrated competitors.

Other:

A fourth category of hot-strip mills encompasses those rolling specialty-steel sheets, coil plate, or skelp to feed their own welded pipemaking operations. Their steel is melted mainly in electric furnaces and they employ continuous, semicontinuous, or reversing mill configurations. Given their role as niche producers, they generally do not compete with mills in the first three categories.

Outlook for Minimill Competition

Of the 67.6 million annual tons of hot-strip mill capacity currently in place, some 4.5 million tons can be regarded as "minimill capacity." It is accounted for by Nucor's two mills and those operated by Beta, Tuscaloosa, NS Group, and Laclede. Tuscaloosa rolls purchased slabs into coiled plates on a reversing mill, and the electric-furnace steelmakers NS Group and Laclede both roll strip mainly to supply their own welded pipemaking operations. Nucor and Beta roll sheet products for sale, the former at two thin-slab installations and the latter using purchased slabs until its plans for an electric-furnace melt shop and caster are carried to completion.

Nucor and Beta are both recent entrants into the flat-rolled business, although the routes taken by each to establish production capability have been decidedly different. Nucor gained market entry by pioneering new technology, namely, thin-slab casting, whereas Beta purchased an existing hot-strip mill from Alpha in the United Kingdom for installation at Portage, Indiana. Nucor's first flat-rolled plant went into operation at Crawfordsville, Indiana, in 1989 and was followed by its second such plant at Hickman, Arkansas, in 1993, while Beta's relocated hot-strip mill came on line in 1992.

The advent of thin-slab casting dates back to 1986, when SMS Concast, having tested its invention, proposed it to Nucor. The demonstrated ability of the two Nucor mills to successfully commercialize the technology has been a primary catalyst in spurring both the development of alternative thin-slab technologies (See technology section) and considerable interest on the part of other potential entrants into the flat-rolled business. Nucor's first thin-slab plant at Crawfordsville gave rise to announcements by other minimills that they too would be entering the business, perhaps not with the same technology, but by combining novel approaches to slab casting and hot-strip rolling with the management and operating techniques common to minimills.

New Jersey Steel, for example, planned to install a Krupp/Platzer high-reduction mill starting with 3–5 inch slabs, in contrast to Nucor's 2-inch slabs, while Birmingham Steel planned a joint venture with scrap supplier Proler International and Italian plantmaker Danieli to convert the former Baytown, Texas, plant of United States Steel to produce sheet products. These and other minimill plans made at the peak of the steel cycle in 1988–89 never materialized, in part because of the lean years that followed. However, within the last year or so, as the steel market has improved and Nucor has successfully started up its second thin-slab plant, the list of other companies intending to follow Nucor's lead has taken on significant proportions. Only this time announced plans have already started to translate into actual plant construction.

As table 3–12 shows, the list of announcements for new minimill capacity in the flat-rolled business is headed by Nucor itself, which is presently enlarging both Crawfordsville and Hickman by an aggregate 1.9 million tons. In the first-quarter of 1994 the former's hot-coil capacity will increase from its current annual level of 1.0 million tons to between 1.8 and 1.9 million tons, and shortly thereafter the latter's capacity will go from 1.2 million tons to between 2.0 and 2.2 million tons. In addition to the Nucor expansion, construction is presently underway at the Co

Table 3–12
Flat-Rolled Capacity of U.S. Mini-Mills:
Existing and Announced
(millions of net tons)

Existing Capacity:	
Nucor/Crawfordsville IN	1.00
Nucor/Hickman AR	1.20
Beta/Portage IN	0.80
Tuscaloosa/Tuscaloosa AL	0.65
NS Group/Wilder KY	0.56
Laclede/Alton IL	0.25
Total	4.46
Announced Capacity:	
Nucor/Crawfordsville IN	0.90
Nucor/Hickman AR	1.00
CoSteel-Dofasco/Gallatin KY	1.00
Beta/Portage IN	0.80
Ipsco/Midwest	1.00
Nucor-Oregon/West Coast	1.00
USS-Worthington	2.00
North Star	1.00
Birmingham	1.00
Chaparral	0.80
Steel Dynamics/Midwest	1.00
Total	11.50

Steel-Dofasco joint-venture plant at Gallatin, Kentucky, which is scheduled to bring its first-phase capacity of 1.0 million tons on line at the beginning of 1995. Plans call for a second phase, boosting capacity to more than 2.5 million tons, to be ready for start-up sometime in 1997.

The 2.9 million tons of new capacity now under construction will give minimills the combined ability to roll 7.4 million tons of hot coils, and while it is most uncertain, if not improbable, that all of the other announced minimills listed in table 3–12 will be built, they represent projects for which firm plans have been drawn up or which their respective companies presently have under active study. Taken together, the listed announcements represent 11.5 million tons of potential, new hot-strip-mill capacity; second-phase expansions already being considered would see another 3.5 million tons of capacity put in place.

Considering that the 67.6 million tons of hot-strip mill capacity already in operation is more than adequate to satisfy the market's requirements for hot-rolled coil through the year 2010, the prospect of installing another 15.0 million tons of capacity raises some crucial questions about the future impact of minimill competition. If new, excess capacity is to be built, will existing capacity be forced to shut down? Will market share be taken away from imports? What are the implications for the price structure in the flat-rolled market and for the industry's long-term profit outlook?

For some time to come, the competitive impact of minimills on the flat-rolled business will be influenced by their limited product capabilities given current technology, initially focusing their participation toward the low end of the market. However, because the vast majority of all hot-strip mills roll products sold for low-end application, new minimill entrants will draw business away from most other flat-rolled producers.

Most affected, of course, will be existing mills that rely heavily on selling low-end product, including some of the smaller integrated mills and the minimills themselves, as well as foreign suppliers to the low-end market. Notably, if all the announced minimill projects and their second-phase expansions are seen through to completion, the minimills would have some 19 million tons of flat-rolled capacity and would be capable of supplying more than 80 percent of the market's low-end requirements.

In time, as the flat-rolled technology minimills employ progresses in its evolutionary development and becomes adapted to producing midrange and even some high-end products, minimills will have a more widespread competitive impact. Whatever flat-rolled market segment they seek to enter, however, the limited growth potential of demand and the existence of more-than-adequate supply capability portends a business in which extremely tough competitive conditions are likely to prevail on a long-term basis.

Comparative Cost Trends

The degree of competitive resistance encountered by minimill sheet producers will depend in significant part on the ability of integrated mills to attain comparable costs as a means of reinforcing their entrenched advantages in product quality, value-added processing, and diverse customer support services. Minimills have the potential to realize cost savings from their use of electric-furnace steelmaking, thin-slab casting, nonunion labor, and a general business culture characterized by such traits as simple management structures and incentive pay.

According to one estimate, the potential operating-cost advantage accruing to a minimill, in this case Nucor, versus a low-cost integrated mill, in producing low-end sheets during the second quarter of 1993 amounted to $35/ton for hot-rolled coils and $70/ton for cold-rolled coils. The estimate recognizes a "significant difference" in the products offered, including the better and thinner gauges rolled by the integrated mill, and it must also be recognized that the margins are susceptible to the vagaries of the scrap market, particularly in view of the limited availability of low-residual scrap that minimills need to support flat-rolled production.[11]

As a growing list of minimill sheet producers tap into the low-residual scrap supply, upward pressure will be exerted on scrap prices, and even more so when scrap is in heavy demand. Likewise, minimill steelmaking costs will increase over time as efforts to move up the quality scale necessitate the use of direct-reduced iron or some other ironbearing charge material as a tramp-element dilutent. The marketing of upscale sheet products will also entail the added cost of customer-support services. And finally, the future availability and cost of purchased electric power and the disposal of electric-furnace flue dust are also likely to raise minimill steelmaking costs.

Integrated mills will also experience upward pressure on a number of flat-rolled cost components, but, compared to minimills, will have a much wider range of opportunity to effect additional cost reduction. After cutting costs and raising productivity significantly since the mid-1980s, integrated mills are continuing their efforts, both by reconfiguring and updating their plants and by changing restrictive work rules as permitted under recently concluded, cooperative labor agreements. In time, integrated mills themselves will move to implement thin-slab casting, particularly as improved versions of the technology are successfully commercialized, which is likely to happen within the next three to five years.

Indicative of the cost-cutting strategies still open to integrated mills is LTV Steel's recent reconfiguring of the west side of its Cleveland, Ohio, integrated plant. The changes are centered around a new $312-million direct-hot-charge complex (DHCC) installed to link an existing and recently upgraded basic-oxygen steelmaking shop and an existing second-generation hot-strip mill with a new ladle-met station and new continuous-slab caster. The DHCC complex displaced an outmoded ingot-casting and slab-rolling operation, and in so doing reconfigured Cleveland-West to conform to minimill-type operating conditions, permitting steel to be processed from the caster to hot bands in about one hour, with a labor input of some 0.7 hours per ton, which is on a par with that attained by minimills.[12]

To achieve this productivity, Cleveland-West, represented by the United Steelworkers Union, uses a nontraditional work system specifically designed by employees and management for the new DHCC complex. A special labor agreement covering the work system provides for flexible work assignments and specified efficiencies. Operating personnel, for example, perform or assist in maintenance, and operations are continuous, with no equipment shutdowns for shift changes or other labor interruptions. Provision is made to adjust worker compensation based on the resulting plant performance. In many respects, methods more nearly comparable to those of minimills provide for just how labor is to be scheduled and compensated.

Estimated operating-cost savings from the DHCC complex are in the area of $100 million annually, and LTV management is convinced that the complex is capable of delivering hot-rolled coils at costs competitive with those of minimills using thin-slab casters.

Outlook for Thin-Slab Casting

Thin-slab casting, like conventional continuous casting in the initial stages of commercialization, has so far proven to be a minimill technology. However, as previously noted, thin slabs are already being applied by Nucor to support hot-rolled coil production in the 2-million-ton range, an output volume more characteristic of integrated mills than minimills, and, in fact, a number of integrated mills presently have thin-slab projects under active study. This makes it likely that over time, particularly as refinements in thin-slab casting make it possible to produce high-quality sheets, including the grades used in automobile bodies, the technology will disseminate across the industry into both minimills and integrated mills, and be used by the latter to complement and possibly eventually displace the conventional thick-slab casters presently in place.

The installed base of conventional slab casting, virtually all of which is within integrated plants, supports hot-strip mills that are more than adequate to meet market demand over the next fifteen or more years. In many cases, the casters represent significant financial commitments recently made by integrated producers to remain competitive in what for many is their sole remaining business. And this is why new minimill entrants to the sheet market will encounter tough competitive conditions. However, it does not mean that thin-slab casting is destined to be a largely redundant steel technology.

The history of technological progress in steel is replete with examples of new production methods displacing conventional technologies, even when the latter had an installed base of capacity more than adequate to meet market demand. If capacity already in place precluded the dissemination of new technology, then the open-hearth furnace would never have been displaced by the basic-oxygen furnace, nor ingot casting and primary rolling by continuous casting. Whether or not thin-slab casting will come to rank as a similar breakthrough technology must await further progress in its development. However, if and when it is shown that thin-slab casting affords significant advantages in lowering costs and increasing product quality across a broad spectrum of required steel grades, it may well displace conventional casting, just like the BOF supplanted the once-revered open-hearth furnace.

Thin-Slab Casting in Europe and Japan

In both Europe and Japan there is considerable interest and activity in installing new minimills to produce flat-rolled steel, even though there is excess steel capacity generally and, as in the United States, sufficient steel-producing capacity to meet the market's needs for many years to come. At present, European hot-strip mill capacity totals some 98 million annual tonnes, with 86 million tonnes located in what were Western countries and 12 million tonnes located in the former Eastern bloc, but the combined operating rate on this capacity ran at less than 70 percent over the last few years. In Japan, hot-strip mills representing 62 million tonnes of capacity have been operating at 79 percent.

Against this backdrop of excess capacity, the installation of new thin-slab casters will ultimately depend on the cost and quality advantages the new technology affords. This, as already noted, will also be true in the United States, as it will in other steel-producing countries. However, in Europe and Japan other influences are likely to forestall the technology's introduction by limiting the construction of new minimills to produce flat-rolled steel. In the European Community, the High Commission's efforts to reduce capacity will make it difficult to obtain permission to build additional minimills with federal or state funding, and in Japan most leading minimill companies that would be candidates for thin-slab casters are subsidiaries of integrated flat-rolled producers that are disinclined to add new sheet capacity.

Europe currently has 1 million annual tonnes of thin-slab capacity, divided equally between Arvedi's carbon-sheet plant at Cremona, Italy, and Avesta's stainless-sheet plant at Avesta, Sweden. Although Arvedi has drawn up plans for expanding its plant, and thin-slab projects have been studied by companies in Belgium, Germany, the Netherlands, Spain, and Turkey, the possibility of minimill sheet facilities spreading to become a competitive threat to European integrated producers is by no means as great as it is in the United States, not with the High Commission in Brussels calling for a 30-million-tonne reduction in EC capacity. Obtaining required High Commission endorsement for publicly supported new-plant construction will remain difficult, at least for the next several years. However, this does not preclude private-sector investments in thin-slab casters, a number of which are likely to be installed.

Germany has thus far been the hub of innovation in thin-slab casting, with commercial processes having been developed there by Schloemann-Siemag (SMS), inventor of Nucor's technology, and Mannesmann Demag Huttentechnik (MDH), which together with Finarvedi invented Arvedi's technology. Also in Germany, development work is currently being conducted by Thyssen at Duisburg on what would become the next generation of thin-slab casters. Participated in by Usinor and SMS, the work has progressed to the pilot-plant stage and has successfully cast slabs in thicknesses of one inch or less, compared to the two-inch slabs cast by Nucor, the purpose being to minimize subsequent rolling requirements and so too capital costs. Encouraged by the pilot plant's results, Thyssen is now considering construction of a commercial plant that would come on line as early as 1996 and, according to current company estimates, would be capable of reducing its finished steel costs by $30–$60 per tonne.

Although a minimill built by Thyssen to commercialize the company's thin-slab technology would be privately owned and not require High Commission approval, another proposed thin-slab caster at Ekostahl, a former East German steelmaker being restructured with German government assistance, must meet EC conditions for reducing capacity before it can proceed. Expectations are that a thin-slab facility is likely to be built at Ekostahl's Eisenhuttenstadt plant after Riva SpA of Italy completes its intended Ekostahl acquisition.

Another possible European mill, a 1.5-million-tonne unit that has been ordered but is currently on hold, is planned for installation at Izmir, Turkey, by Cukurova Celik Endustrisi, and if built would use the thin-slab technology developed by MDH-Arvedi. Turkey has seen its raw-steel ouput grow from 2.5 million tonnes in 1980 to more than 10 million tonnes, and being outside the European Community, faces no restrictions on its capacity, which has been expanded over the last decade in significant part by constructing a number of minimills. Currently, Turkey's sheet production is accounted for by integrated producer Eregli Demir ve Celik Fabrikalari (Erdemir). The Cukurova project would significantly increase sheet capacity, as would another thin-slab project that has been considered by integrated producer Turkiye Demir ve Celik Islemeleri (TDCI).

Turning to Japan, nearly all of the country's minimills, of which there are some forty-five, are either too small to fund investments in the sheet business, or are controlled by major integrated producers that already have ample sheet-producing capacity. Two large minimills are independent of integrated producers, namely, Tokyo Steel and Yamato Steel, both of which produce wide-flange beams. Tokyo, however, has entered the hot-rolled sheet market by constructing a minimill that employs electric-furnace steelmaking and a conventional continuous caster. The mill's current production is between 800,000 and 1 million tonnes annually, which is to be expanded to 1.5 million tonnes. While it is conceivable that Yamato may enter the flat-rolled business, the company has thus far expressed no intention of doing so.

Competition between Tokyo Steel and integrated producers for the sheet business is very limited, since Tokyo's sheets are based on electric-furnace steel refined from scrap charges containing contaminants. The company's sheet operation competes principally with sheet and strip imports that have reached several million tonnes in recent years. In 1992, for example, Japanese imports of wide strip and cold-rolled sheets totaled 2.4 million tonnes and 661,000 tonnes, respectively, much of which is targeted at the low end of the flat-rolled market, wherein Tokyo Steel has become a strong competitive force.

Tokyo and Yamato both produce considerable tonnages of heavy structurals. In this market segment they have become competitive with Japan's integrated mills. Leading integrated producer Nippon Steel, for example, which previously had a very large percentage of the structural business, has had its market share reduced.

An interesting development has taken place recently in Japan as Kawasaki Steel is rolling hot coils from steel made in an electric furnace by Daiwa Steel Company. The electric furnace is located near the Mizushima Works of Kawasaki. Steel from this furnace is shipped to Kawasaki's continuous caster where it is cast into slabs that are further processed on its hot-strip mill. The coils produced are not of the highest quality but will compete with imports. The steel is made from Kawasaki's mill scrap and, when necessary, some of Kawasaki's pig iron. Thus, the product is of acceptable quality and at a competitive cost with blast-furnace iron and BOF steel. Further, it gives Daiwa Steel an opportunity to run its electric furnace at full capacity.

4
Substitute Materials

Steel has encountered competition from other materials in a number of applications over the past two decades. Until recently, steel enjoyed the enviable position of replacing other materials for a number of applications, particularly in the container and appliance industries. In the container industry, the material replaced was glass, and in appliances, particularly in the ice box that predated the refrigerator, it was wood as the refrigerator replaced the ice box. Wood also suffered in certain types of construction where steel beams replaced heavy wooden beams.

Over the past two decades other materials have begun to invade what was long considered to be steel's domain. The principal materials that are being substituted for steel are plastics, aluminum, cement, and ceramics. The areas invaded include the automotive industry, construction, the container industry, and appliances. These challenges have provoked a response from the steel industry that has involved considerable research activity as well as significant capital investment.

Automotive Industry

The automotive industry has been a principal, if not the leading, consumer of steel in all the industrialized countries where automobiles are produced. This is particularly true of the United

States, Japan, Germany, France, Italy, the United Kingdom, and Spain. Further, the automobile industry has been a growing one in the post–World War II era. In 1970 some 29.4 million vehicles were produced worldwide. This figure rose continually with few interruptions until it reached 49 million vehicles in 1989. There has been a slight decline since, to 47.4 million vehicles in 1992.

Steel shipped in the United States and Japan to the automotive industry in 1992 was 11.1 million tons and 10.9 million tonnes, respectively. This represents a considerable drop in steel use by the automobile industry in the United States. In 1973, with a production of some 12.7 million vehicles, steel shipments were 23.2 million tons. In 1992 production was 9.8 million vehicles, a drop of 2.9 million, or 23 percent, while steel shipments fell by 52 percent to 11.1 million tons. This was due principally to downsizing vehicles, a major trend in the United States in the late 1970s. The same situation did not occur in Japan, where there was no appreciable downsizing; as the number of cars increased, steel shipments also increased (see table 4–1).

The principal reason for downsizing the cars made in the United States, and also the main reason for substituting other materials for steel, was to reduce the weight of the automobile so that it could obtain more miles per gallon of gasoline, and thus reduce air pollution by a significant amount. To accomplish this goal, steel was reduced in the production of the automobile so that the total weight of the average car was likewise lowered.

The argument for replacing steel with plastics and aluminum is that these two substitute materials are lighter and consequently reduce the weight of the automobile. However, since this program to reduce automobile weight was inaugurated in the late 1970s, the steel industry has improved its product by reducing the weight and thickness of the steel, while at the same time maintaining its safety qualities. Further, because of the reduction in automobile size, it is no longer necessary, in most instances, to use an automobile frame on which the body was

Table 4–1

U.S. and Japanese Automobile Production and Steel Shipments to the Automotive Industry, 1970–90

	U.S.		Japan	
	Automobile Production[a]	Steel Shipments[b]	Automobile Production[a]	Steel Shipments[b]
1970	8.3	14.5	5.3	4.1
1971	10.7	17.5	5.8	3.5
1972	11.3	18.2	6.3	4.7
1973	12.7	23.2	7.1	6.1
1974	10.1	18.9	6.6	5.6
1975	9.0	15.2	6.9	5.5
1976	11.5	21.4	7.8	6.5
1977	12.7	21.5	8.5	6.6
1978	12.9	21.3	9.3	7.3
1979	11.5	18.6	9.6	8.5
1980	8.0	12.1	11.0	9.5
1981	7.9	13.2	11.2	8.8
1982	7.0	9.3	10.8	8.5
1983	9.2	12.3	11.1	8.6
1984	10.9	12.9	11.5	9.3
1985	11.7	13.0	12.3	10.0
1986	11.3	11.9	12.3	9.2
1987	10.9	11.3	12.3	9.2
1988	11.2	12.6	12.7	10.8
1989	10.9	11.8	13.0	11.6
1990	9.8	11.1	13.5	12.2

Sources: Motor Vehicles Manufacturers Association, *Facts & Figures '91;* Japanese Automobile Manufacturers Association, *Vehicle Statistics for Japan;* Japan Iron and Steel Federation, *Monthly Reports of the Iron and Steel Statistics;* American Iron and Steel Industry, *Annual Statistical Report.*

[a] Millions of units.
[b] Millions of tons.

built. The body itself now became the frame, and this has reduced car weight appreciably.

Since steel shipments to the automotive industry are so vital to the health and profits of the steel industry, any intrusion of significant proportions by another material poses a serious threat. This is particularly true of steel sheets, which constitute the bulk of shipments to the automotive industry. In the United States, for example, in 1992 total shipments of hot-rolled, cold-rolled, and galvanized sheets produced amounted to 39.8 million tons; of this total, 8.5 million, or some 21 percent of output, were consumed by the automotive industry.

Some advance has been made by both aluminum and plastics in substituting for steel in automobile production. In the United States, for example, the amount of aluminum used in the average automobile in 1980 was 130 pounds. This increased to 177 pounds by 1993. The use of plastic composites rose from 195 pounds in 1980 to 243 pounds in 1993. This is a relatively small percentage growth considering a period of thirteen years. However, the producers of both aluminum and plastics are hard at work to extend their products' usage in the automobile industry in the future.

As a consequence, this has inspired a program on the part of the steel producers to combat the challenge of these two materials, not the least of which is the organization of a number of committees involving participation from both the automotive and steel industries in almost every phase of automotive design and production. Figure 4–1 presents the committees established to create the Auto/Steel Partnership Program.

The partnership between the steel and automotive industries was extensively described in a paper delivered by Edmond Pachura, chairman and chief executive officer of Sollac, at the International Iron and Steel Institute meeting held in Paris on 4 October 1993. He described the situation as it exists in Western Europe. The partnership extends to services, materials, processes, and design, and details the work that has been accomplished in these various areas.

The contest between aluminum and plastics on the one side and steel on the other has been in evidence for some ten years. As indicated, aluminum has not increased very much in terms of actual pounds used in automobiles from 1980 to 1993, and the same is true of plastics.

A number of articles have appeared in the trade press indicating the possible future developments in both aluminum and plastics usage. Many of these are optimistic projections and de-

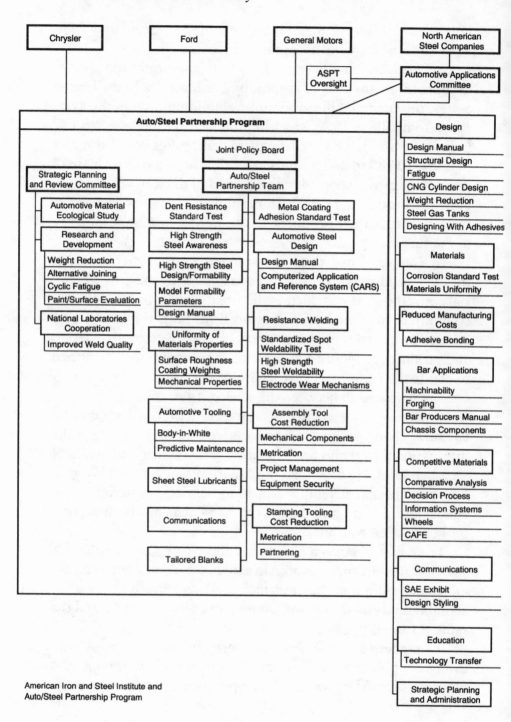

American Iron and Steel Institute and
Auto/Steel Partnership Program

pend to some extent on announcements made by any one of the "Big Three" automobile producers, Ford, Chrysler, or General Motors.

The pressure is constantly on to reduce vehicle weight. Aluminum seems to have the edge over plastics at the present time in terms of its acceptability and the fact that it is 100 percent recyclable; plastics are not nearly so recyclable, although a great deal of effort is being expended to improve their recyclability.

The developments in aluminum, as described in the Pachura paper, indicate that in relation to aluminum, there has been a great deal of discussion but not much activity in terms of its use in the automobile body. Sample automobiles have been made using aluminum, but none of these have reached the production stage.

An attempt on the part of the steel industry to reduce car weight has extended to the complete design of the automobile, rather than just to reducing the weight of individual parts. This is known as an holistic approach. It treats the entire vehicle rather than its separate parts. Thus, the complete design in terms of the use of steel has been examined and will result in a weight reduction of 140 pounds and a savings of $40 per unit. The steel industry maintains that the use of design strategies can reduce the weight of an average automobile just as effectively as substituting plastics or aluminum for steel in certain parts. For example, as indicated previously, a gradual reduction in the size of cars permitted the use of the automobile body itself as the structural member replacing the heavy steel frame on to which the body, drive train, and suspension are attached. The use of the body in this respect is called the monologue design concept, which allows the exterior skin to become the structural member, permitting the virtual elimination of a heavy automobile frame with a corresponding reduction in weight.

By 1982 almost all of the high-volume vehicles were converted to monologue construction. With monologue construction, the steel body itself performs all three of the major functions required of a modern automobile: styling, structural integrity, and crash energy management. Thus, steel, with a change in design, eliminated a significant amount of average automobile weight, which in turn permitted a higher mileage per gallon of gasoline.

The contest between steel and plastics and aluminum will continue because the plastics- and aluminum-producing companies have set their sights on obtaining more of the automotive market and have hopes of increasing their percentage significantly. However, there was no major growth in the use of plastics and aluminum between 1980 and 1993, as is indicated by the relatively small growth in terms of the number of pounds of both plastics and aluminum used by car manufacturers. The program to reduce car weights even more will continue for the remainder of the 1990s, but thus far steel seems to have more than held its own as the key material used by the automotive industry. However, a continuing challenge to steel's predominance must be met with constant striving on the part of the steel industry for better and lighter steels as well as changes in automobile design that will permit the use of less overall material, including steel, plastics, and aluminum.

Indicative of the challenge and the battle being waged among plastics, aluminum, and steel for the automobile market is the number of articles on this topic published in the trade press. In fact, one magazine, the August 1993 issue of *Iron and Steelmaker,* carries three articles, each immediately following the other, extolling the virtues of aluminum, plastics, and steel. The first article, entitled "Aluminum and Automaking: Its Time Has Come," points up the advantages of aluminum in its applications in automobile construction. The second article, "Plastics—Better than Ever," pleads the cause for plastics in the automotive industry. The third article, "Steel—Back in the Driver's Seat," details the progress steel has made in recovering part of its market from other materials. Another article by Peter Peterson[13] in *Metal Forming* (November 1991), entitled "Steel, Not Plastics, Reduces Auto Weight—A Myth Dispelled," points up the advantages gained from steel particularly in view of the improvements made in steel products over the last decade.

One of the measures of success achieved by one material or the other is the amount used and the increases in that amount over a period of years. *Ward's Automotive Yearbook for 1993*, in discussing materials used in the construction of automobiles, gives details on the quantities (in pounds) involved over a period of thirteen years from 1980 to 1993. Table 4–2 offers a picture of materials usage.

Table 4–2 makes evident the reality that although aluminum and plastics have made large percentage gains, the amount of material is limited, whereas steel is overwhelming. It is also evident from the table that the amount of steel per vehicle has declined. However, this is part of the program to make the automobile lighter, so that, although steel is declining to reduce the weight of the cars, the increase of other competitive materials is not very significant in terms of pounds, yet it is to some extent in terms of percentage.

Edmond Pachura, chief executive of Sollac, states: "We are constantly hearing about the decline of steel in automobile construction but this is far from the whole truth. First, let us define our terms: if we mean that the weight of steel in vehicles is decreasing, then this is true, and the trend will continue. But if one claims that other materials are in the process of replacing steel in the structure, the body panels, and under the hood, then we are simply wrong."

Another factor in the use of steel for automobiles is the recyclability of the three materials in question. Aluminum and

Table 4–2
Materials Usage in the Automotive Industry, 1980–1993

	1980	*1985*	*1990*	*1992*	*1993*
Steel	1893.5	1740.1	1563.52	1709.5	1726.5
Iron	484.0	469.0	398.0	429.5	411.5
Aluminum	130.0	138.0	158.0	173.0	177.0
Plastics	195.0	211.0	222.0	245.0	243.0

steel are completely recyclable, whereas many plastics present problems, so much so that in Germany the difficulty of removing plastics and sending them to a landfill has given scrap dealers pause.

Construction

Construction has been one of the largest markets for steel throughout this century. In fact, it has rivaled the automotive industry in terms of steel consumption for decades and still does. In 1988, U.S. steel shipments to the construction industry were 12.1 million tons, while those for the automotive industry were just a bit more, at 12.6 million tons. In 1990, construction surpassed the automotive industry with 12.1 million tons versus 11.1 million tons and thus became the leading steel consumer in the United States.

The principal competitor of steel in the construction industry is reinforced concrete. This material has made considerable inroads into the U.S. steel market since the end of World War II. In the 1930s most of the high-rise office buildings were constructed with structural steel. This applied to buildings ten stories or higher. However, in the postwar period, because of the limited amount of construction activity during the depression years of the 1930s and the war years of the early 1940s, there was a tremendous demand for construction because of the fifteen-year period of inactivity when very few high-rise commercial or residential buildings were built. At the close of World War II, there was a strong revival in construction of virtually all types of buildings. Literally millions of square feet were planned and built.

The high rate of activity made strong demands on construction materials, including steel, and there just was not enough to go around. Further, in 1959, there was a lengthy steel strike and delivery times were relatively long. As a consequence, architects and construction contractors looked to other materials, and the one that was most favored was reinforced concrete. A consid-

erable amount of research undertaken by the producers of concrete added strength to this material. Its advantages were
strongly promoted by the cement industry, with many trained
engineers working in the field with architects on specific
projects. This was the situation in the United States.

In England, the same condition existed, particularly in London. After World War II the steel industry was unable to provide material for the construction boom and the concrete
industry moved in to supply the growing market. In Britain,
steel frames for nonindustrial projects were virtually abandoned
due to the shortage of steel and its consequent high prices relative to those of concrete. In the 1980s British steelmakers organized a program in an attempt to reverse the situation. The price
of steel was reduced, in some cases by as much as 35 percent.
Further, a group was formed consisting of steel producers and
fabricators to canvas and persuade architects and engineers to
use fabricated steel. The program brought about a decided
change in the use of steel by 1991, with some 50 percent of the
construction market using this material.

The reasons for the change were summed up by Gordon
Sambrook of British Steel Corporation in a paper delivered at
the International Iron and Steel Institute meeting in Berlin in
October 1989. He said two reasons accounted for the switch to
steel for multistoried buildings:

> First, the most important, was a drastic change in the price relation-
> ship of basic materials. In the last decade, increased productivity in
> Europe's steel industry has reduced real prices by a third without a
> corresponding reduction in concrete products. The second reason is
> because of a major market development campaign led by British
> Steel's steel engineering team working closely with our fabricator
> customers and supported by technological developments such as . . .
> wraparound blanket fire protection systems.

In the United States since 1980, a situation has developed
between the use of steel and the use of reinforced concrete that
has stabilized the use of both materials. In the construction of

industrial buildings from 1980 through 1992, the amount of steel used during most years was well over 50 percent. This was true from 1980 to 1985, from 1987 to 1989, and again in 1992. The amount of steel used during those years varied from a high of 57 percent in 1982, to a low of 51 percent in 1992. In 1986, 1990, and 1991, the percentages fell below 50, reaching a low point of 40 percent in 1986.

With regard to commercial buildings, the steel market share was somewhat less than in industrial buildings. It ranged from 37 percent in 1990 to 43 percent in 1991, crossing the 50 percent mark in 1992, and again for three-quarters of 1993 when it ranged between 52 and 57 percent.

In office buildings, steel's share was in the high 50 percent range from 1980 to 1993 with the exception of one year, 1991, when steel's share fell to 43 percent. In residential buildings, steel did not fare nearly as well as in other types of buildings. In 1980 steel accounted for 19 percent of total material used. During the remainder of the 1980s, steel's share was in the 20–29 percent range, falling back to 18 percent in 1991, and then increasing to 43 percent in 1992.

Table 4–3 illustrates average steel usage, for all types of buildings, from 1987 to 1993.

One area of growth that could be very significant in the future is residential construction, where steel has moved into a building sector long dominated by wood.

Table 4–3
Percentages of Steel Consumption for All Building Construction in U.S., 1987–1993

Year	Percentage
1987	42.7%
1988	43.0%
1989	42.6%
1990	39.5%
1991	43.0%
1992	51.0%
1993[a]	51.8%

[a] The percentage for 1993 is for first three quarters only.

During the Chicago World's Fair, "The Century of Progress" in 1933, steel-frame homes were placed on exhibition. United States Steel also formed a subsidiary called United States Steel Homes in the 1960s. However, the ideas for constructing steel residential buildings did not catch on at the time, since artisans, principally carpenters, did not have any experience with handling steel and no educational materials were available. Further, lumber was cheaper than steel.

Subsequently, however, pre-engineered metal buildings did gain a degree of acceptance, as did the use of steel framing. Engineers, construction workers, and architects have become accustomed to working with steel studs, which have become a preferred material for use in such buildings as hospitals, office buildings, and shopping malls.

Steel had an advantage in Japan, particularly in Tokyo where land is very expensive and new home builders demand larger buildings. The solution was found in building upward three and four stories where wood did not have the strength to sustain these heights.

In the United States in early 1991 a task force was formed as an advisory group to the American Iron and Steel Institute to research the possibilities for using steel in residential construction. The group enunciated a vision, a mission and a target:

The *vision* was to have steel as a material of choice for North American residential construction.

The *mission* was to create an environment that enabled and encouraged the practical, economic, and widespread use of steel in residential construction.

The *target* was to have steel studs, joists, and trusses used in 25 percent of new residential construction within five years.

Several subgroups were also formed, including education and promotion; technology and research; codes, specifications, and standards; and market research and economics. Meanwhile, the competing material, namely, lumber, was increasing in price, thus creating an opportunity for steel.

The National Association of Home Builders conducted a survey on the West Coast of the United States in January 1993. Some 6 percent of the respondents indicated an interest in steel framing as an alternative to lumber. By midyear, in the face of increasing lumber prices, the same question brought a 45 percent response favorable to steel. This is particularly due to lumber prices which had increased to the point where steel's use resulted in significant savings for a relatively modest home. In 1992, there were 500 homes built using steel for framing. In 1993, the count had risen beyond 10,000.

The primary product used in home construction is hot-dipped galvanized steel. About 5 tons of steel are used in a 2,000-square-foot house versus 20 tons of lumber. The aim of the American Iron and Steel Institute advisory group is to have 1,500,000 tons of hot-dipped galvanized steel used in the residential market by 1997. It is evident that a large number of home builders will be using steel framing. Under these circumstances, the market could become the largest end-use market for coated steel, with a potential usage of about 5–7 million tons each year. This may not occur for another five to ten years, but most steel people are optimistic. If these projections are realized, there will be a need for more galvanizing lines to fill the demand. The projections are optimistic and even enthusiastic and it remains to be seen if they will be fulfilled in the time allotted.

The Andrew Estates South Project will result in the construction of two hundred homes over a two-year period in Florida City, which was almost completely destroyed by Hurricane Andrew. These homes will use steel for framing, roofing, and some siding. The project will receive widespread publicity and could do much to promote the use of steel in residential construction. This is an example of the steel industry taking the offensive rather than remaining on the defensive to ward off challenges from other materials.

Recently, in 1990, the steel industry undertook a program to install steel in place of wood in the construction of residential homes. The outlook for the future is quite optimistic: the industry expects that by 1997, 350,000 units will be built using steel as a building component. The amount of steel that would be consumed when the operation reaches its height could reach 5–7 million tons. The National Association of Homebuilders has indicated that steel could be the building material of the future. By 1997, it is expected that the market will be 1.5 million tons, on its way to a projected figure of 5–7 million tons by the year 2000.

Containers

The market for containers has twice witnessed a major change in the materials from which they are made during the last century. The first change was from glass to tinplate which formed tin cans that were used for the packaging of fruits, beverages, food, and what are known as general-line cans, including paint, powders, chemicals, and the like. Tinplate dominated the field for several decades. In fact, by 1960, it was used overwhelmingly as a container material.

Tinplate is a product that is over 99 percent steel with a thin coating of tin. In recent years black plate and tinfree steel have been used in the production of a large portion of cans and containers.

Over the past three decades there has been a decided drop in the shipment of tinplate, from 6,201,000 tons in 1965 to 3,682,000 tons in 1990. Black plate sales reached 458,000 tons in 1965, but sales fell to 270,000 tons by 1990. Tin-free steel, a relatively new product, accounted for an annual production of 900,000 tons and 960,000 tons during the span from 1980 to 1989. The decline in tinplate sales is due to the loss of the beer and soft-drink can markets: today 96 percent of the cans for these markets are made from aluminum. The beer and soft-drink markets constitute a major share of the overall can market.

Another invasion into cans and containers has been made by

plastics. This is particularly true of the large drum container as well as the one-quart oil container. In 1992, a total of 130 billion cans were produced; of these 130 billion cans, some 93 billion were made for beverages, both beer and soft drinks. Of this total, 89 billion cans were made of aluminum and 4 billion were made of tinplate. Aluminum has virtually taken over the beverage can business. One of the leading reasons for this takeover is the recyclability of aluminum. Currently, the aluminum industry recycles 63 percent of its cans. Steel is at 40 percent, but the industry is making a concentrated effort to raise this figure to 66 percent. To this day, attempts made by tinplate to reclaim a portion of the beverage can market have been relatively unsuccessful.

Of the cans produced in 1992, some 32 billion were intended for food use. Steel held over 95 percent of this market. Attempts made by aluminum to enter the food can market have been quite unsuccessful.

Two consortia have been formed by steel companies to develop steel cans to take back part of the beer and soft-drink can business. A European consortium involves British Steel, Hoogovens, and the tinplate division of Thyssen, and another consortium involves Nippon Steel of Japan, Weirton Steel of the United States, and Usinor of France. Both consortia are striving to develop a lighter tinplate; to date they have succeeded in developing a tinplate that is approximately 25 percent lighter than that which was made before.

In the United States, the challenge is very strong judging by the fact that 96 percent of the beer and soft drink can business is taken by aluminum. In other countries around the world, there is a decided difference. In Japan, aluminum has about 50 percent of the beverage can business, in Europe some 40–60 percent, and in France particularly, a very low percentage of aluminum versus steel.

Tinplate seems to have a dominant share of the food-can market and to some extent the general-line cans. Whether a portion of the beer and soft-drink market will be reclaimed, particularly in the United States, is a matter for future development.

About 800,000 tons of steel are used in pails and drums in a year. This figure has held fairly steady for the last few years, although the manufacture of these items has increased by about 5–10 percent a year. Thus, steel has lost out in terms of the growth factor. In drums, some 33–35 million are produced per year, ranging in size from 16 to 85 gallons. Seventy-five percent of these are 55-gallon drums. In addition, there are 40 million reconditioned drums.

Appliances

Appliances include such products as refrigerators, freezers, ranges and ovens, clothes washers and clothes dryers, dishwashers, food waste disposers, trash compactors, room air conditioners, and dehumidifiers. Steel shipments to the U.S. appliance industry have been reasonably constant since 1983, as table 4–4 indicates. Table 4–4 details the tonnage of steel shipped as well as the number of appliances produced.

Table 4–4 portrays a significant increase in the amount of appliances produced year by year since 1983. In 1983 37,417,000 units were produced. Units produced increased to a peak of 50,653,000 in 1987, and thereafter declined moderately to 46,226,000 units in 1992. Steel shipments between 1983 and 1992 declined from 1,618,000 tons to 1,503,000 tons, having reached a high point in 1989 of 1,721,000 tons. Consequently, with the growth in appliance unit production and the decline in steel shipments to the industry, there has been a loss of position to competing materials, particularly plastics.

During the 1980s the plastics industry made a particular effort to contact the appliance manufacturers with the purpose of working with them in terms of the use of materials to help the manufacturers to reduce the costs of finished units. This gave the plastics manufacturers an entrée into the appliance business that has been considerable. The amount of plastics shipped to the appliance industry increased significantly during the 1980s. Be-

Table 4–4
Appliance Market Statistics

Year	Steel Shipments to Appliance Market[a] (000) Tons	Appliance Shipments to End Market[b] (000) Units
1983	1,618	34,417
1984	1,635	41,558
1985	1,466	44,020
1986	1,648	47,585
1987	1,633	50,652
1988	1,638	50,033
1989	1,721	49,461
1990	1,540	45,623
1991	1,388	43,080
1992	1,503	46,226
1993	1,559 Est.[c]	46,239 est.
1994	1,583 Est.[c]	46,486 est.

Note: Major home appliances are defined as refrigerators, freezers, ranges and ovens, clothes washers, clothes dryers, dishwashers, food waste disposers, trash compactors, room air conditioners, and dehumidifiers.

[a] Source: American Iron and Steel Institute, *Annual Statistical Report, 1992.*

[b] Source: Association of Home Appliance Manufacturers, *1993 Major Home Appliance Industry Fact Book.*

[c] Source: AISI Committee on Commercial Research.

tween 1987 and 1992, the pounds of plastics in appliances increased for approximately 1 billion pounds to 1.150 billion. This increase at 150 million pounds, represents an annual growth rate of 3 percent. Projections for plastic use by 1997 are as high as 1.370 billion pounds, which represents an annual growth rate for plastics use between 1992 and 1997 of some 3.5 percent.

In the 1990s various steel companies have taken an active position contacting appliance manufacturers. They have worked with them in terms of design and materials use in order to improve final cost of the appliances. Steel has a definite position in the appliance industry. In fact, Frigidaire, which manufactured 20 percent of all refrigerators sold in 1991—a total of 7.9 million units—has concentrated on steel as a manufacturing material. It has even used steel for the liners of the units.

Part of the decrease in steel consumption by the appliance

manufacturers is due to the use of lighter steels in the various appliances. The steel industry has always had a strong position with the appliance manufacturers. With the new programs the industry has recently put into operation whereby the steel industry consults with the appliance manufacturers on design as well as use of materials, steel should maintain its present position. However, there is no doubt that competition from plastics will continue into the years ahead.

5
The Steel Mill of the 21st Century

T he last quarter-century has seen major advances in steel technology, leading to widespread changes in the physical characteristics, component facilities, and operating practices of both large-scale integrated steel plants and their generally smaller, nonintegrated counterparts. The overall objective of these technology-induced changes has been to increase the speed and efficiency and to lower the costs of producing steels that meet ever-more-exacting quality standards, with the additional provision that the production process be made compatible with environmental-protection and worker-safety requirements. Directed at this overall objective, the ongoing evolution of technological change will result in the steel mill of the future or, considered from a longer-term perspective, "the steel mill of the 21st century."

Future Advances in Steel Technology

The purpose of this chapter is to assess the possible direction of future advances in steel technology to gain insight into the mill of the 21st century. It will be examining the major divisions or stages of steel-industry operations, from basic materials preparation through ironmaking, on through the melting of raw steel for subsequent casting and rolling into finished steel products. Historically, most of these major operating stages, which are set forth in Figure 5–1, have been comprised of multiple, batch-type production activities, resulting in numerous interruptions of their process flows and equally numerous instances of stocking in-process inventories. Imposed by the limits of available technology, this batch-type approach has placed limits on levels of attainable operating efficiency and has involved heavy capital and environmental-cost burdens; it has contributed to yield and energy losses; it has created conditions susceptible to the development of production bottlenecks; and it has restricted coordination between and among the major operating stages.

Given the limits and difficulties imposed by traditional, batch-type production, many of the major advances in steel technology have been directed at rationalizing process flows to permit an increasing degree of continuous operation. This technological emphasis is exemplified in continuous casting, continuous hot and cold rolling, and continuous annealing, all of which have replaced less-efficient, batch-type operations. The ideal steel plant ultimately would permit a continuous flow of production from start to finish. In projecting prospects for the mill of the 21st century, one can safely conclude that many of the technologies it incorporates will have the capability to bring this "ideal" much closer to reality. The changes made in the years to come will involve both physical facilities and operating methods and will be directed at the following general areas:

- Use of computer-based systems to coordinate functions within and between the major stages of production and to eliminate or minimize production bottlenecks and permit process flows that are more nearly continuous.
- Elimination of batch-type operations through the adoption of new, technologically advanced production practices and facilities.
- Modification of facilities and production techniques to speed production, improve process yields, and conserve energy.
- Adoption of methods for producing cleaner steels with more exacting chemical specifications.

Steel Production Process Flows

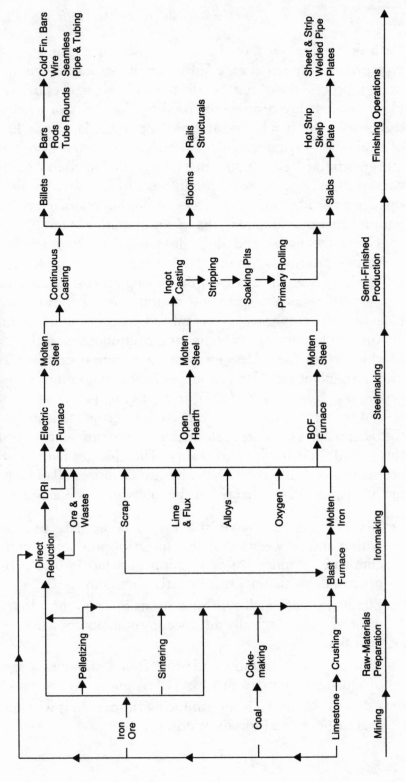

- Automation of production processes and the application of robotics, particularly in areas of product inspection and quality control, to achieve improved labor productivity and lower production costs.
- Streamlining of individual-plant product lines to eliminate low-volume items and permit longer, more-efficient production runs.

With respect to coordinating steel plant operations, the future will witness widespread implementation of computer-based systems to increase production efficiency by monitoring and controlling facility operations and to schedule inventory flows in a comprehensive and balanced manner that integrates every stage of the production process. The many batch-type operations that occur in a steel plant give rise to multiple requirements for synchronizing diverse production activities to optimize final-product output in a manner consistent with varying levels of steel demand.

Although computerized scheduling and control can contribute to the efficiency of all steel plants, the evolution on a major scale of new, continuous technologies can occur only over a protracted time frame, encompassing periods of laboratory experimentation, pilot-plant testing, initial commercialization, and—finally—full commercial dissemination and application. Judged by past experience with already established continuous technologies, such as the continuous hot-strip mill and continuous casting, the time frame involved can amount to as much as two decades. Of course, technological changes, such as those involved in modifying facilities already in place, generally are commercialized over a much shorter period of time.

While the steel plant of the future will become more highly computerized and automated, it will also become more specialized in its product concentration. The benefits of specialization have been demonstrated by the "minimill" approach to steel production, so much so that its success has started to impact investment planning and technology utilization in larger plants operated by major steel companies. The tendency in recent years has been for minimills to become larger and more sophisticated in their operations, and for larger plants, including those that are fully integrated, to become somewhat smaller and more selective in the finished steels they produce.

In scaling down fully integrated, multiproduct plants, one approach has been to eliminate blast-furnace operations, with corresponding changes at the steelmaking and finishing stages, the end result being to narrow the product mix and reduce the overall volume of finished-steel production. The attraction of circumventing the blast furnace derives from the avoidance of difficult, batch-type operations, including cokemaking and sintering, both of which involve heavy capital expenditure requirements and produce difficult environmental-control problems.

To date, electric-furnace steelmaking has been the primary means of avoiding or scaling down blast-furnace dependence, although its use as a scrap-based process with a 100 percent scrap charge significantly limits the range of its product application. Even the highest quality purchased scrap contains residual-alloy tramps in amounts that exceed the upper limits specified for high-quality carbon steels and even for many of the medium-quality carbon grades. It is extremely important to limit the residual-alloy content of drawing-quality steel, which is used extensively for cold-forming applications, and although raw steel heats with higher-than-preferred tramp levels can be used for some drawing-quality steel production, this usually requires longer annealing times and closer attention during hot working. In addition to posing problems for continuous annealing, this increases the rate of product rejection and, consequently, unit production costs.

Besides turning to electric-furnace steelmaking, steel companies have tried to reduce blast-furnace dependency by utilizing ironmaking by direct reduction (DRI) and various modifications of the basic-oxygen steelmaking process (BOF) to permit its increased scrap utilization. The former approach has found significant acceptance at locations where abundant supplies of low-cost natural gas are available to fuel the most technically advanced production methods, while the latter approach is still in the early stages of its commercialization but will likely come into more widespread use in the years ahead.

In considering the steel mill of the 21st century, one's focus of attention is naturally drawn to the impact of energy sourcing and availability, particularly since steel production is so energy-intensive. Indeed, one of the major thrusts of current capital expenditure programs in the steel industry is toward achieving energy conservation. One of the prime advantages of the blast furnace is its utilization of coal-based energy, accompanied by the cogeneration of coke-oven gas to fuel a variety of steel mill operations. Conversely, direct reduction's high degree of dependence on natural gas has retarded its widespread adoption, while electric-furnace steelmaking faces constraints imposed by the availability and cost of purchased or generated electricity.

Given energy's pivotal importance to steel, any major, long-term shift in worldwide energy supplies relative to steel's demand requirements could radically alter the future direction of changes in steel technology. Development of a limitless source of low-cost electricity, for example, would speed the blast furnace's phase out and accelerate a conversion to electrical processing in every phase of steel mill operations. Most of the precise technologies that steel mills would implement in such a conversion remain for future discovery, as do the precise scientific solutions that one day will permit the construction of commercial reactors to produce electricity by nuclear fusion. However, the evolution over many years of ways and means to perfect fusion energy will undoubtedly occasion the introduction of facilities incorporating lasers, plasma torches, or some alternative means of directing high inputs of electrical energy to speed production in what by then will be the steel mill of the 21st century.

Moving from the general to the specific, the balance of this chapter discusses the more significant, evolving changes in steel technology that can be perceived from our current perspective.

The discussion reviews technological changes at each of the major stages in the steel-production process, in effect providing a catalogue of plant and equipment items that may be incorporated in the steel mill of the future.

Raw Materials Preparation

The need for steelmakers to meet more-demanding quality standards will require greater attention to raw materials preparation, particularly as scrap continues to be substituted for virgin iron units, not only by integrated mills seeking to shore up their constrained ironmaking capabilities, but also by new minimill competitors who will initiate scrap-based sheetmaking operations. Quality steel requires quality scrap and iron inputs, which means that more attention will have to be paid to scrap processing and to securing adequate supplies of blast-furnace coke and other ironmaking raw materials.

As steelmakers demand higher quality scrap, increasing use will be made of advanced methods of scrap identification and grade classification, together with the use of more extensive sorting and sizing procedures. More extensive use will also be made of the heat from process off-gases to increase the temperatures of scrap prior to its charging in the steelmaking furnace. Environmental-control requirements will prompt increases in the preparation and reuse of iron-bearing steel-plant wastes, involving the use of extraction, agglomerating, and concentration techniques both at the steel plant and at outside facilities.

In the longer term future, plasma energy may well be used at iron ore mines to reduce and smelt ore, so that high-grade iron, not ore, will be shipped from the mines to steelmaking plants. Such an advance in raw materials preparation would help facilitate direct steelmaking by permitting more precise control of the required chemical reactions by separating them from the process of combustion.

Integrated steelmakers will continue to face increasing difficulty in sustaining their coke-making operations and will continue to work on developing alternative technologies to produce either iron or steel directly by means of coal instead of coke. However, because none of the noncoke alternatives can reasonably be expected to challenge the blast furnace as the preeminent ironmaker for many years to come, integrated steelmakers will first make greater use of more immediate technological approaches to reduce their need for coke. These technologies include the substitution of iron, improvements in blast-furnace efficiency, and pulverized coal injection (PCI) to provide a near one-to-one replacement for a portion of the blast furnace's coke input.

United States

In the United States environmental regulations will require a major investment in coke ovens to meet clean air standards. These currently relate to a number of items including leakage in coke-oven doors. In 1993, this was reduced to 8 percent and by 1998 must be 3 percent. The percentage figures are based on the number of doors that are allowed to leak. In a 100-oven battery, for example, 8 percent means that no more than eight doors are allowed to leak. By 1998, this will be reduced to three doors.

Achieving these objectives, as well as others, will require a significant steel industry investment. In fact, in 1990, when the Clean Air Act amendments were passed stipulating these standards, it was estimated that to replace or repair the total U.S. coke-oven capacity of 27–28 million tonnes in existence at that time would require an investment of $4–6 billion. Since then, a number of batteries of significant size have been closed, including the batteries at the Sparrow Point plant of Bethlehem Steel Corporation and a battery at Inland Steel. In the case of Inland, the closed battery was a victim of stringent federal environmental regulations and damage suffered by the battery that was too expensive to repair. The cost of completely rebuilding the battery was estimated at $150 million.

With the cost of installing or rebuilding coke-oven batteries, plus the difficulties that have arisen in meeting environmental requirements, a number of companies in the United States are considering the use of PCI at the blast furnace. The amount will be in the area of 350–400 pounds per net ton of iron. Use of PCI will reduce the amount of coke required by approximately 30–35 percent, and thus reduce the need to rebuild or replace a number of batteries. The capital investment required to use coal injection is considerably less than that required to increase coke-making capacity, perhaps as little as one-third the amount. Consequently, the total estimated investment to keep U.S. coke-making capacity in line with future steelmaking requirements will be reduced somewhat, from $4–6 billion to approximately $3–3.5 billion.

But many coke-oven batteries, will still need to be replaced. This problem has caused concern among steel companies due to the limited availability of capital to finance such a large investment. The most recent example of a complete rebuild is at the Great Lakes plant of National Steel, where a battery was rebuilt that will provide some 900,000 tons of coke at a cost in excess of $300 million. These figures have caused concern among U.S. integrated steel producers in regard to the replacement of aged or noncompliant coke facilities.

In the United States, coke capacity has declined drastically since 1973, from approximately 58 million tons to some 23 million tons at present. Of the 79 batteries that are operating today, about 40 or 50 percent are over thirty years of age. Since some operable batteries are not functioning, batteries more than thirty years old actually contribute about 40 percent of current capacity. These batteries will have to be replaced during the 1990s if this level of capacity is to be maintained. The Clean Air Act amendments of 1990 have specified regulations on emissions that will render a significant portion of the industry's capacity noncompliant. Thus, the U.S. steel industry needs to replace batteries because of both advanced age and noncompliance with environmental regulations. But according to present plans of the integrated steel companies in the United States, not all of the batteries currently in existence and operation will be replaced.

Coal injection is new to the United States: only one blast furnace had it in operation during the past ten years. Currently, another PCI unit is under construction at the Gary steel works of United States Steel, and a third has been contracted for at the Indiana Harbor plant of Inland Steel. A number of other companies are actively considering PCI facilities. Conversion to PCI facilities will reduce the need for coke throughout the U.S. industry by a significant amount, perhaps as much as 3–4 million tonnes. However, in order to provide sufficient blast-furnace feed for the U.S. industry, a number of coke-oven batteries will have to be rebuilt or replaced. This will present a difficult financial problem, but one that must be solved.

European Community

In the EC, of the 57 million tonnes of coke capacity, approximately 19 percent of producing batteries are over thirty years old, with 10 percent being between twenty-six and thirty years old, and another 8 percent being between twenty-one and twenty-five years old. This means that more than one-third of EC coke capacity will require replacement or significant repair by the turn of the century. The principal steel producers—Germany, Great Britain, France, Italy, and Belgium—have batteries of similar age among their coke-oven facilities.

In **Germany,** capacity is 17.7 million tonnes. Thirty percent of the coke-oven batteries are thirty years old, and another 13 percent are twenty-one to thirty years old. By the year 2000 replacement requirements should cover some 42 percent of German coke capacity. Here, environmental regulations, as previously stated, call for the installation of dry quenching, which requires a multimillion dollar investment. The installation of coke facilities represents a large capital investment. Recently, a 2-million-tonne plant completed by Ruhrkohle, which included dry quenching, required a capital investment of $800 million. Thyssen contemplates the possibility of installing a 2.5 million-tonne plant for an estimated $700 million. The estimated cost of a 1-million-tonne plant with by-product facilities and dry quenching is approximately $375 million. The battery by itself, including dry quenching but without the by-product plant, costs in the area of $270 million.

The German industry has for some time injected pulverized coal, in some instances as much as 350 pounds, per tonne of iron with trial rates of up to 400 pounds. Other plants have operated with as much as 250 pounds, while some plan to initiate PCI at 200–230 pounds. Consequently, with the current use of coal injection, not as much of an advantage will be obtained in Germany with increased injection rates as in the United States, where PCI is just starting to be utilized. Any increase in PCI in Germany will not replace as much coke as is contemplated in the United States, where very little coal injection is employed at the present time.

Great Britain has a coke capacity of 9.2 million tonnes. Some 19 percent of Great Britain's coke-oven batteries are more than thirty years old, and another 15 percent are twenty-one to thirty years old. Consequently, by the year 2000, there should be a replacement of some 34 percent of British coke capacity. British Steel Corporation, which operates all the blast furnaces in Great Britain, and consequently uses the vast portion of the nation's coke, has developed a coal-injection process that it is applying to a number of its blast furnaces. In one instance, as much as 400 pounds of PCI is used, per tonne of iron produced and in others considerably less, although plans have been made to increase the amount. Consequently, some reduction in coke input will be achieved in the years ahead. Meanwhile, British Steel, Hoogovens, and Ilva are experimenting with higher rates of coal injection using a considerable amount of oxygen. Tests are being made on a small blast furnace at Cleveland Ironworks in the United Kingdom.

France has a capacity to produce some 8 million tonnes of coke, the vast portion of which is consumed by Usinor-Sacilor in its principal plants, including Dunkirk and Fos. A relatively small portion of its coke-oven battery capacity, 14 percent, is more than thirty years old. However, an addition 14 percent is between twenty-six and thirty years old, and 10 percent is between twenty-one and twenty-five years old. Consequently, a significant number of the batteries will be candidates for replacement or rebuilding in the late 1990s. The French also use PCI at their furnaces, ranging in amounts from 240 to 300 pounds per tonne of iron produced, with plans to reach 350 pounds at Dunkirk in 1994. The furnaces located at Lothringen are equipped with coal-injection facilities; however, the rates there are less than 200 pounds.

Italy has a coke-oven capacity of approximately 9 million tonnes. With few exceptions, it is used in the plants of Ilva, formerly called Italsider. Of the total coke-oven battery capacity, some 11 percent is more than thirty years old, and another 22 percent is between twenty-six and thirty years old. Thus, a third of the Italian coke capacity will come due for replacement or rebuilding by the onset of the 21st century. The Italians are currently using PCI on a limited number of furnaces to the extent of 200 pounds per tonne of pig iron. However, plans call for an increase in this rate to at least 300 pounds per tonne. If these plans are carried out, coke consumption in Italy can be significantly reduced.

Belgium has a coke capacity of approximately 6 million tonnes, much of which is under the ownership of Cockerill-Sambre and Sidmar, a company of which Arbed owns 67 percent. Of the total coke-oven battery capacity, 30 percent is more than thirty years old, and another 6 percent is between twenty-one and thirty years old. The need to rebuild some coke ovens will arise in the late 1990s. Current coal injection at Belgium's large integrated plants ranges up to 250 pounds; the smaller companies have an injection of some 120 pounds.

The Netherlands has one integrated steel mill, Hoogovens, located at Ijmuiden. Total cokemaking capacity there is 3.4 million tonnes. Forty-two percent of capacity is between six and ten years old; 38 percent is between sixteen and twenty years old;

and a very small 10 percent is more than thirty years old. Consequently, the Netherlands does not face significant coke-oven replacement problems in the next ten years. Its only problem can arise from a change in pollution regulations. Coal injection on one of its two blast furnaces has reached as high as 420 pounds per tonne of iron. However, this was achieved in an unusual trial; the normal rate is closer to 310 pounds per tonne. The limitation seems to be in the grinding plant, and its expansion could lift the PCI rate to slightly over 400 pounds per tonne of iron.

Spain has a relatively small coke capacity of some 3.3 million tonnes. Its two integrated companies, Ensidesa and Altos Hornos de Viscaya, consume virtually the total amount. The industry is fairly young and consequently has no coke ovens over thirty years old, and only 5 percent of the capacity is between twenty-six and thirty years old. Most of its capacity, approximately 50 percent, is in the eleven-to-fifteen-year range. Spain is currently restructuring its industry: there are plans to shut down a number of blast furnaces and replace them with electric furnaces. There are no plans for coal injection and the need for coke is expected to decline.

Japan

The Japanese steel industry is a development of the postwar period, with most of its capacity installed in the 1960s and 1970s. Consequently, a large percentage, approximately 44 percent, of its coke ovens are between twenty-one and twenty-five years old. By the years 2000 to 2005, many of these batteries will be scheduled for replacement, since at that time approximately 45 percent of the batteries will be more than thirty years old. With this replacement prospect facing the Japanese industry, all of the integrated companies and the Japanese Iron and Steel Federation joined together in 1987 to develop the DIOS process for making iron without coke.

If successful, the DIOS process will provide a means of avoiding the large expense of replacing many of Japan's coke ovens between 1999 and 2005. The joint effort plans involves seven years of experimentation, scheduled to be completed in 1993 or 1994, at which time the best results of all the participants will be combined to produce a pilot or demonstration plant. Thus, the industry hopes to avoid having to fully replace its aged coke capacity around the turn of the century. Thus a number of replacements that would have been scheduled for introduction as early as 1999 to 2005 have been put on hold. The success or lack thereof of the DIOS process will determine the extent of coke-oven rebuilds in the Japanese steel industry in the years ahead.

The Japanese have adequate coke capacity, more than 52 million tonnes at the present time. In fact, Misubishi Chemicals operates a coke-oven battery in order to obtain chemical products; in a sense, coke is a by-product and is sold in the export market at reasonably low prices.

Regarding coal injection, Japan has been using it since the early 1980s to replace oil, which increased in price in the late 1970s. Most Japanese blast furnaces are equipped with facilities for coal injection. However, the amounts injected have been relatively small, consisting of 100–140 pounds per tonne of iron produced, with the exception of Kobe Steel which uses over 200 pounds. Plans are underway to increase Japan's injection rates.

PCI Outlook

As this review of the plans of most individual countries reveals, coal injection at the world's blast furnaces will increase significantly in the years ahead. Current PCI technology places the upper limit at some 400 pounds per tonne. Although a number of blast furnaces will likely attain this maximum, the average utilization rate will probably be somewhat less than 300 pounds. As a consequence, PCI could eventually displace about one-third of blast-furnace coke requirements. However, the significance of this potential on the future coke demand–supply balance must be evaluated in relation to the already high rates of PCI being utilized in many ironmaking countries, particularly those in the EC. Furthermore, if less coke is charged into the blast furnace, coke strength must be improved to support the burden, which increases coking times and therby reduces coke-oven throughput.

Since coke will continue to provide upward of two-thirds of the fuel and reductants needed to sustain world blast-furnace operations, the fact that much of the world's coke-oven capacity is aging beyond critical limits provides cause for concern over the adequacy of future coke supplies, particularly during periods of peak ironmaking and steelmaking activity. There is a strong possibility that by the mid- to late-1990s coke will be in short supply, since many oven batteries due either for replacement or major repair have not been scheduled for rebuilds. The high cost of installing or rebuilding new ovens plus the impact of increasingly stringent environmental standards have been curtailing and will continue to curtail the steel industry's capital investments in coke-making capacity.

Although the worldwide coke supply is today more than adequate, a number of companies are woefully short of coke. Indeed, some must purchase all they require. Despite coal injection and the possible development of alternative methods of making iron outside of the blast furnace, a large number of batteries must be rebuilt or replaced if the industry is to sustain its iron-making operations in the years ahead.

As of now, with plentiful supplies of coke available on the world market, the urgency in rebuilding ovens is not very immediate. However, as more ovens go down—and many will be closed over the next few years—the coke supply situation will tighten, resulting in a probable increase in price from current world-market levels.

In the 1980s imported coke was available in the United States for $86 a ton delivered to the East Coast. Many U.S. companies decided it was cheaper to buy coke than to manufacture it. As a consequence of such decisions, the demand for purchased coke increased considerably and the price went up to $120 a ton. National Steel Company had been considering a plan to close the aged coke ovens at its Great Lakes plant and not replace them in view of the low price of imported coke. However, once the price increased, the company changed its mind and invested over $300 million in rebuilding a large coke-oven battery. This procedure could well be followed by a number of steel companies throughout the world in the remainder of the 1990s and into the 21st century.

In those cases where the required capital investment is considered too large for some steel companies, joint ventures could be formed to spread the investment cost. There will be relatively few such joint ventures, however, and this increases the possibility that coke may be in short supply.

Ironmaking

At the ironmaking stage of production, the years ahead will see technological progress, directed not only at advancing the capabilities of the dominant blast-furnace process, but also at commercializing alternative ironmaking methods that use both solid-state and smelting reduction to transform iron ore into steelmaking iron. The opportunity for added blast-furnace improvement will be restrained insofar as many blast furnaces have already pushed the limits of process and operating efficiency in terms of such variables as high blast temperatures, supplemental fuel injection, and burden preparation. This means that most future changes in ironmaking technology are likely to involve direct-reduced iron (DRI) and iron-carbide production, smelting with coal instead of coke, and the various approaches to "direct" ironmaking/steelmaking.

Two interesting developments of a kindred nature are now in progress: one is Fastmet, which is a means of producing direct-reduced iron and the other is the iron-carbide process. The Fastmet process was developed by Midrex Direct Reduction Corporation. It converts iron oxide fines into metallic iron using pulverized coal or other solid carbon-bearing materials as a reductant. The product that results is direct-reduced iron in either pellet or briquette form, which can be used in electric furnaces, blast furnaces, or other steelmaking facilities. Fastmet offers a product that is ideal for supplying the low-residual iron required to produce clean steels by diluting scrap contaminants. The actual preparation of the material is accomplished with a mixture of iron ore concentrate, a pulverized reductant (coal, coke, or char), and a binder. All of these are mixed together and pulverized. The pellets are dried to remove moisture and next fed into a rotary hearth furnace. The pellets are then rotated while being heated to 1250–1350°C, a process that reduces the iron ore to metalic iron.[14]

Iron carbide produces a product that is a fine material consisting of 93 percent iron and 7 percent carbon, introducing reformed natural gas into iron fines. This product is intended primarily for use in the electric furnace. It can also be used in the basic-oxygen converter. Its function in the electric furnace will be to dilute contaminants in scrap so that the resultant steel will be cleaner and can be used particularly in the formation of steel sheets from electric-furnace steel. It will provide sheet steel that will have better drawing qualities for various applications.

The iron-carbide process is now in the pilot-plant stage; however, a $60 million investment is being made by Nucor in Trinidad to build a first plant that will manufacture some 350,000 tonnes of iron carbide for inclusion in the charge in Nucor's electric furnaces at Crawfordsville, Indiana, and Hickman, Arkansas. Nucor is also planning a joint venture with Oregon Steel to build a 1-million-ton plant on the West Coast of the United States, which will use either iron carbide or DRI as part of the furnace charge.

In terms of new technology for integrated plants, there has been a concentration in the ironmaking segment of the industry. The Corex process, which produces iron from a mixture of iron ore and coal, is in operation in South Africa at ISCOR. This is a small plant with about a 300,000-tonne annual capacity. Another Corex plant is being constructed in South Korea; it will produce 1,600 tonnes a day, for a total of 600,000 tonnes a year. Voest-Alpine, the manufacturer of this process, is currently working on a plant with a capacity of 1 million tonnes annually; such a plant may be installed at LTV Steel at its Cleveland plant in the United States. This will produce iron as well as an abundance of gas that can be used to generate electricity.

The considerable offgases generated by Corex must be used apart from the process itself. Thus work is underway on other coal-based smelting technologies that postcombust their offgases to supply process energy. Projects to develop such "direct" smelting alternatives to the blast furnace have been underway in Europe, Australia, Japan, and the United States. The major shared technical objectives of all the projects is efficient postcombustion and heat transfer to advance the smelting reduction of iron ore.

In November 1993, at Kwinana, Western Australia, CRA Ltd. of Australia and United States–based Midrex Corporation commissioned a $140-million research and development facility aimed at the scale-up and commercialization of the HIsmelt process for direct iron-ore smelting. HIsmelt originated in Germany in 1982, when CRA and Klockner tested smelting reduction in a 60-tonne oxygen steelmaking converter and subsequently built a small-scale pilot plant at the Maxhutte Steelworks in southern Germany, where trials were conducted from 1984 to 1990. HIsmelt injects noncoking coal, hot prereduced iron oxide, flux, and hot air into a reactor vessel containing hot metal. It transfers the energy produced during combustion of the coal to the molten metal and uses the reactor's exit gases to prereduce iron ore in a circulating fluid bed. The purpose of the Kwinana project is to scale up HIsmelt to an hourly smelting capacity of 15 tonnes.

In the United States, a cooperative development project is being pursued by several U.S. and Canadian steelmakers and universities under the sponsorship of the American Iron and Steel Institute (AISI) and the U.S. Department of Energy (DOE). The North American initiative, called the Direct Steelmaking Project, was launched in 1988 and has seen the construction of a pilot facility at Universal, Pennsylvania, near Pittsburgh, where smelting rates of several metric tonnes per hour have been attained while producing iron or semisteel. In the AISE-DOE process, a vertical bath smelter containing molten metal and slag is charged with coal and partially reduced iron-ore pellets and blown with oxygen. Combustion of the coal supplies the energy for smelting reduction of the ore, and the offgases are postcombusted in prereducing iron-ore pellets to wustite in an integral shaft furnace. Plans call for scaling up the process by constructing a plant capable of smelting 300,000 tonnes of iron annually.

Japan's effort at developing a blast-furnace alternative involves a cooperative steel industry and government project termed the Direct Iron Ore Smelting, or DIOS, Project. It has been underway since 1988 and involves participation by the Japan Iron and Steel Federation, the Coal Mining Research Center of Japan, and the eight major Japanese integrated steel producers. DIOS makes direct use of noncoking coal and a sinterlike iron-ore feed in a single reactor vessel in which molten slag serves as the smelting medium. In the project's initial stages, which ran through 1992, the participants worked independently on various of its assigned aspects; since that time, the focus has been on coordinating their findings, the objective being to build the first production unit within the next one to two years. The strategy is to have a blast-furnace alternative available by the turn of the century, when many of Japan's coke-oven batteries will be coming due for rebuilding or replacement.

Steelmaking

The steelmaking stage of production will undergo continuing technological change as the BOF and electric-furnace processes are upgraded and modified, ladle-metallurgy facilities become more widely adopted, and more advanced methods of metallurgical analysis are employed. Over the longer term, ongoing experimental programs to achieve one-step or direct steelmaking will move toward commercialization, their objective being to combine the current batch-type operations involved in coke-making, blast-furnace ironmaking, and conventional steel-making.

Given the developing constraints on blast-furnace hot metal, integrated steelmakers with basic-oxygen steelmaking furnaces will be inclined to modify their operating practices to increase scrap usage up to the maximum 30 percent or so of the charge that can be tolerated by the conventional, top-blown process. The availability and price of good-quality scrap will govern the extent to which this occurs, as well as the extent to which steel-makers adopt combined blowing (from top and bottom) and granulated coal injection to increase scrap usage to 40–60 percent of the furnace charge. Other process and practice modifications can increase BOF scrap utilization to 100 percent, significantly increasing process flexibility. The years ahead will also see dynamic process control and slag-free tapping more widely applied.

The electric-arc furnace, the principal melter of scrap, will continue to undergo improvements aimed at enhancing its efficiency, conserving energy, and reducing electrode consumption. Offgas utilization for scrap preheating, coal injection with oxygen, and direct-current melting will find wider acceptance. To date, two technologies have been successfully commercialized to modify the electric furnace for scrap preheating and continuous melting, namely, the Consteel process and the Fuchs Systemtechnik shaft furnace, both of which capture offgas energy to reduce electric power requirements.

Consteel uses furnace offgas to preheat its scrap in a horizontal tunnel through which the scrap is continuously conveyed, whereas the Fuchs process incorporates a vertical preheating shaft into the furnace roof. Consteel has been commercialized by Nucor in the United States and by a number of other steel-makers, and Fuchs units are presently operating at two locations, Det Danske Stalvalsevaerk (DDS) in Denmark and Sheerness Steel Company, Ltd., in Kent, England. Commercial experience has shown that using offgases to preheat scrap by the

Consteel and Fuchs approaches results in average savings of some 25 percent in electric power consumption per tonne of molten steel produced and also reduces electrode consumption at a comparable rate.

The electrode savings realized by scrap preheating and continuously charging are based on melting in alternating-current (AC) furnaces with three electrodes. Electrode savings are also being attained by displacing AC furnaces with direct-current or DC furnaces, most of which employ a single electrode from which the electric arc is transferred via the scrap charge and molten heel to a return anode in the base of the furnace. Recently installed DC furnaces incorporate the melting advances made over decades of AC furnace operation; their commercial use has been spurred on by advances in solid-state power thyristors for AC-to-DC rectification.

Although installation costs for DC furnaces are higher than those for AC units of comparable capacity, the former afford a number of potential advantages. Because DC furnaces generate less electrical noise or flicker, they can be supported by grid systems with low short-circuit capacity; and because they generate less operating noise, they can conform to in-plant noise regulations without being enclosed. Power consumption in melting tends to be lower, in part because a molten heel is retained between heats, and refractory wear is also lower given the increased distance between the single electrode's arc and the furnace perimeter. Finally, DC furnaces afford electrode savings in the 50 percent range, accounting for both materials and change labor.

In time, the electric furnace, whether AC or DC, may well evolve into a hybrid process in which coal and other fossil fuels are used directly to supplement purchased electric power and therby improve overall energy efficiency. Limited use has already been made of the Energy Optimizing Furnace or EOF, commercialized in Brazil by Willy Korf and based entirely on using coal instead of electricity. This and similar approaches to scrap-based steelmaking could become more widespread with advances in process control and offgas utilization. Likewise, the direct ironmaking technologies reviewed above may well be extended to truly make direct steelmaking a commercial reality.

Whatever the steelmaking process, however, one thing is certain: it will be employed mainly as a melting system. Most of the world's steel-refining requirement will continue to be carried out in ladle-refining units. Ladle refining is synonymous with a number of recent entries in the steelmaker's lexicon, including ladle metallurgy, ladle treatment, and secondary refining, and encompasses a wide variety of steel-processing techniques from ladle and stream-vacuum degassing, to wire and particle injection, to gas and induction stirring.

Some ladle-refining systems incorporate heaters and others do not, although more typically heaters are employed in what are known as ladle furnaces, which make it possible to separate the melting and refining phases of steelmaking, in turn, to effectively coordinate primary melting in the basic-oxygen and electric-arc furnaces, which are batch processes, and the continuous forming of semifinished shapes in continuous casters.

In serving the clean steel revolution, ladle refining is used for a variety of purposes: to desulphurize, to deoxidize, to remove inclusions, to closely control chemistry and temperature, and—with vacuum degassing—to remove hydrogen and produce low-carbon steels. Its role in providing batch-to-continuous coordination in the flow of production is indispensable in attaining the design throughputs required for high-production continuous casters, for, regardless of melting delays, the casters are assured of a steady supply of clean, consistently heated steel.

In terms of productivity gains and measurable costs savings, ladle refining improves the operating efficiency of steel plant facilities both upstream and downstream in the flow of production. Upstream, ladle systems boost productivity in the electric-arc and basic-oxygen steelmaking furnaces by limiting their role primarily to melting.

The positive impact on melting-furnace productivity is reflected in the recent installation of a ladle refiner to replace one of the two electric-arc steelmaking furnaces at a plant that was short of steelmaking capacity. The result, even with one melting furnace displaced, was to increase the plant's ability to supply refined steel to its continuous caster by some 20 percent, therby eliminating the need to purchase semifinished sections at a significant cost penalty.

Further upstream benefits from ladle refining derive from reduction in lining wear per ton of throughput in both the electric-arc and basic-oxygen furnaces; the BOF also benefits from enhanced process flexibility in selecting charge materials, since ladle refining permits it to melt a great proportion of scrap versus blast-furnace hot metal. This can enable the steelmaker to take advantage of cost differentials between scrap and hot metal during periods when scrap prices decline and also affords a means of alleviating hot metal shortages that have become increasingly common due to blast-furnace outages or a lack of adequate coke-oven capacity.

Finally, in terms of upstream benefits, ladle refining results in a more efficient use of alloys, with high levels of recovery and close chemical analysis, thereby reducing the cost of alloy additions.

Downstream, the major productivity gains and cost savings from ladle refining derive from its ability to provide batch-to-continuous coordination between steelmaking and continuous casting, thereby unlocking the full design potential of high-speed casting machines, which in recent years have attracted much of the steel industry's investment capital.

Working together, ladle refining and continuous casting supply a steel plant's rolling and finishing facilities with semifinished sections that are higher in quality than could have been imagined when semis were rolled from ingot-cast steel or processed through continuous casters without ladle refining. Combined with advances in rolling mill technology, the clean steel semis have resulted in quality improvements that have sharply improved steel mill yields and cut customer rejection rates on the steel products they receive.

In terms of future development, ladle refining will continue to be intimately tied to continuous casting. The synchronization between furnace and caster will require more and more ladle furnaces. This facility will allow the steel furnace to finish the steel at a lower temperature, since it can be maintained at that temperature or even increased through the use of the electrode heater in the ladle furnace, and thus can be kept ready for the continuous caster.

To reap the benefits of continuous casting, as well as its cost-reduction benefits, ladle furnaces will become essential and will constitute an integral part of the steelmaking process in the years ahead.

Thin-Slab Casting

Among new steel technologies, thin-slab casting is currently attracting the most worldwide interest and could ultimately have the greatest impact on the steel industry's competitive structure. Thin-slab casters represent the centerpiece of seven new compact-strip production techniques that have thus far proven sufficiently viable, either commercially or experimentally, to attract significant steelmaker attention. The seven techniques are shown in table 5–1, which lists their developers, locations, and grades of implementation. To date, only two of the techniques, CSP and ISP, have been commercialized to produce carbon steel sheets, with a third, Conroll, produces stainless sheets.

Compact versus Conventional

As the name implies, the "compact"-strip approach seeks to minimize the plant and equipment needed to produce flat-rolled sheets and strip. In so doing, it seeks to lower break-even plant capacity, and so too the capital and operating costs associated with conventional hot-strip mill operations. Heretofore, sheet production has been the nearly exclusive domain of integrated steelmakers and has constituted by far their major product line and primary source of revenue. Their conventional hot-strip

Table 5–1
Leading Compact Strip Production Concepts, 1992

Process	Developer	Status
CSP	SMS/Concast	Commercialized at Nucor, Crawfordsville, Indiana, and Hickman, Arkansas
ISP	MDH/Arvedi	Commercialized at Arvedi, Cremona, Italy
Conroll	Voest-Alpine	Commercialized for stainless at Avesta, Avesta, Sweden; Pilot plant for carbon steel at Voest-Alpine Stahl, Linz, Austria
TSC	Danieli	Government-financed pilot plant in Italy
ECCO	Krupp/Demag	Pilot plant in Germany
CPR	Thyssen	Pilot plant at Thyssen in Duisburg, Germany
TSP	Tippins	Available for commercial installation from Tippens, Pittsburgh, Pennsylvania

CSP, Compact Strip Production; ISP, In-Line Strip Production; ECCO, Economic Compact Mill; TSC, Thin-Slab Conticaster; CPR, Casting Pressing Rolling; TSP, Tippins Strip Process.

mills usually process inventoried and reheated slabs, continuously cast from BOF steel in approximate thicknesses of 200–300mm. These "thick" slabs are first passed through the conventional mill's reversing or multiple roughing stands, numbering as many as six, and then, once a thickness of 25–38mm is achieved, are rolled on the mill's six- or seven-stand finishing train to a minimum thickness of 1.3mm in the finished coil.

The capital costs of installing a greenfield, integrated plant for conventional hot-rolled sheet production vary considerably, depending on where construction is to take place and the specific equipment items designated for installation. The newest such plant, constructed by Pohang Iron and Steel at Kwangyang, South Korea, saw its first phase come on stream in 1987 at a capital cost of approximately $1.8 billion or $750 per tonne of finished hot-rolled sheet. This compares to estimates for comparable plants in other countries ranging upward to $1,000 per tonne, despite provision at Kwangyang for extensive infrastructure development, including major new port facilities.

A reasonable average capital cost for a conventional integrated plant limited to processing 3.5 million annual tonnes of hot-rolled coils is $2.8 billion, or $800 per tonne of finished output. This estimate covers $800 million in land, utility, and infrastructure costs and facility costs totaling $2.0 billion, incurred in the purchase and installation of coke ovens, a sinter plant, a blast furnace, a BOF steelmaking shop, a continuous slab caster, and a hot-strip mill with a reversing rougher, coil box, and seven finishing stands. The hot mill accounts for the single-largest facility-cost component, about $450 million.

In seeking to streamline conventional sheet and strip production, all of the compact-strip concepts in table 5–1 focus their design changes on the same stages of production, starting with the pouring of molten steel, usually melted in an electric furnace, into the caster tundish and ending with the removal of coiled hot-rolled strip from the rolling mill's downcoiler. The concepts vary in the specific continuous casting and rolling technologies they employ, but all are based on casting thinner-than-conventional slabs to reduce rolling requirements, and—at least theoretically—the required number of hot-strip mill stands, a key element in limiting the capital cost involved. In addition, all of the concepts incorporate some method of achieving a more direct linkage between the casting and rolling stages of production, whereby as-cast slab temperatures are largely retained and equalized to effect energy savings.

Concepts versus Reality

To date, the compact-strip plants in commercial production have been successful in meeting their conceptual objectives, namely, minimized plant and equipment requirements, lower break-even capacities, and capital and operating cost savings. The CSP and ISP plants at Nucor and Arvedi are only fractionally the size of their conventional counterparts, employ significantly less capital per tonne of output—generally half or less—and display an ability to effect comparative improvements in operating efficiency. The fact remains, however, that the compact-strip concept is still in the early stages of its development and is continuing to undergo evolutionary changes at both the commercial and pilot-plant levels that may or may not attain the breakthroughs needed to overcome the basic limitations that remain.

What are these limitations? In general, initial commercial experience has revealed both technical difficulties and quality problems, which have tended to push capital requirements above originally projected levels and have thus far limited the range of sheet applications that can be consistently satisfied. Salable, low-cost sheets for selected, noncritical uses are presently being produced by the compact-strip method, but an equivalent alternative to conventional hot-strip production has not as yet become a commercial reality.

As to specific limitations, one of the most important relates to the current designed capability of compact-strip technologies to produce finished hot-rolled sheets in minimum gauges of 1.7–2.54mm versus the 1.3mm attained on conventional hot-strip mills. As already noted, the casting of thin slabs conceptually aims to circumvent the conventional mill's roughing train, which takes thick 200–300mm slabs down to 25–38mm for finished-product rolling. By comparison, current compact-strip concepts continuously cast thin 50–100mm slabs, depending on the dimensions of their casting molds, and except for the ISP and Thyssen methods, which perform additional soft reductions on the liquid-cored slab within the casting machine, deliver slabs for rolling that are at least double conventional thickness dimensions. In other terms, most of the thin-slab technologies thus far devised provide slabs to their associated rolling mills that are considerably thicker than the bars entering the initial finishing stands of conventional hot-strip mills.

The thickness of most thin slabs poses a dilemma for the compact-strip concept at its current stage of development, for either additional rolling-mill stands must be employed to approach the minimum gauges rolled by conventional mills, or a more limited range of lower-value-added, heavier gauge sheet and strip must be produced. While adding mill stands runs counter to the objective of minimizing facility requirements and increases capital costs, settling for a narrower, lower-margined product line limits both the attainable market scope and prospective earnings.

Provision in the ISP and Thyssen designs to produce thinner slabs of some 25mm prior to rolling recognizes and seeks to address the thickness dilemma. Notably, Arvedi's commercial ISP plant at Cremona also incorporates a roughing train of sorts, a three-stand "high-reduction device" to roll its slabs immediately after solidification down to a thickness of 15mm, which permits a 1.7mm sheet to be rolled on the plant's four-stand finishing mill. By contrast, Nucor, which initially produced the heaviest gauge sheets (2.54mm minimum) on its CSP unit at Crawfordsville, opted to add a fifth finishing stand there and to install a six-stand finishing train at its second CSP plant at Hickman, Arkansas.

Quality Considerations

Based on quality considerations other than minimum gauge, the compact-strip concept has thus far managed mixed results, comparing its finished output to that from conventional mills. Positively affecting quality, the internal metallurgical structure of the sheets rolled from thin slabs has proven to have a finer grain size because of the thin slabs' shorter cooling time, about one-fifth that of a conventional thick slab. Also positive, the dimensional tolerance to which the sheets are rolled in terms of flatness and uniformity of gauge across their width are functions of rolling-mill technologies available to both compact and conventional mill operators, and both the Nucor and Arvedi plants have incorporated some of the latest technologies.

Since Nucor's start-up in 1989, its rolling operations have experienced problems with surface defects caused by casting-mold powders and scale being rolled into its sheets. Considerable time and effort has been spent in attempting to prevent these problems from occurring, and equipment modifications, including the installation of additional scalebreakers, have significantly reduced the extent and frequency of the problems, which despite their persistence are considered by the operators to be temporary in nature.

A more basic negative in terms of compact-strip quality derives from the cleanliness and residual-alloy content of the molten steel supplied to the thin-slab caster. All of the notable compact-strip concepts can be operated with either BOF or electric-furnace steel, and although steel chemistry favors the BOF for producing most grades and qualities of carbon-steel sheets, electric-furnace steel has thus far been employed as the exclusive supplier of steel for compact-strip production. Having evolved conceptually as an alternative to conventional mills, which are predominantly tied to the BOF, the compact-strip approach has come to be regarded as a minimill technique, using electric furnaces to avoid the coke making and blast-furnace ironmaking associated with the BOF.

The problem with electric furnaces, however, is that the quality of the sheets and strip produced depends on the grades of ferrous scrap that can be purchased for melting. Unfortunately, even the highest quality purchased scrap (including No. 1 heavy melting, No. 1 bundles, and shredded scrap) contain residual alloys in amounts exceeding the upper limits specified for all but the lower end of the sheet-production spectrum. Since the same quantities of most of these residuals present in the scrap charged will be present in the steel produced, this effectively limits the application of scrap-based steelmaking to sheet and strip production. The problem can be addressed by using DRI to upgrade the electric-furnace charge, which is currently being done by Nucor. However, this adds to operating costs, and if a DRI facility has to be constructed, a minimum of $100 per tonne would be added to the compact strip plant's capital cost.

Compact-Strip Outlook

The compact-strip technique for producing carbon-steel sheet is still in its early evolutionary stages, with only two approaches commercialized to date. There is currently more operational information available for Nucor's CSP plants than for any other plant or concept, including Arvedi's ISP unit, which just recently completed its break-in. This leaves an extremely limited body of experience to draw upon for evaluating the technique. Thus its eventual role awaits future improvements in the technologies involved, which will likely occur over the next several years, as production units incorporating still-to-be-commercialized approaches come on line.

At its current stage of development, the concept has been shown capable of effectively producing a limited range of commercial-grade sheets on a reasonably consistent basis and at competitive costs. Because of the limitations on sheet gauge and other aspects of quality—which, in turn, limit the range of product applications that can be satisfied—the concept cannot as yet be considered an equivalent alternative to conventional sheet production methods. It does, however, afford a viable means of producing certain sheet products within a minimill-type environment in plant configurations generally scaled down to 1 million tonnes or less capacity per year and reducing capital costs to some $400 per tonne.

Much of the difference between the capital needed for compact-strip production and the $800 per tonne or more required for a 3.5-million-tonne conventional, integrated plant derives from using electric-furnace rather than BOF steelmaking, which occasions some of the quality problems characteristic of the compact-strip approach. Finally, it should be noted that the capital costs reported for Nucor and Arvedi may prove to be significantly lower than those realized on future installations, given the fact that SMS and Mannesmann were anxious to build their first plants for promotional purposes, but more importantly because future units are likely to incorporate additional finishing-mill stands and other equipment modifications.

Although the compact-strip concept is compatible with the minimill's operating philosophy, its costs of implementation, however reduced they may be from conventional levels, are nontheless well beyond the funding capabilities of most minimill companies. Thus, at present, the concept permits access to a very limited segment of the overall sheet and strip business.

Compact-Strip Concepts

Each of the leading compact-strip concepts CSP, ISP, Conroll, TSC, ECCO, Thyssen, and Tippens, will be described in turn below, including relevant available information on such subjects as their equipment components, plant layout and dimensions, designed annual capacity, capital investment requirements, manpower needs, raw materials inputs, sheet and strip outputs, and developmental potential. Because of differences in the extent to which each concept has developed and the degree of attention that each has attracted, the information available varies considerably from concept to concept and so too the descriptions that can be presented.[15]

Compact-Strip Production (CSP). The CSP or compact-strip production concept is based on the designs of Schloemann Siemag AG (SMS) in Germany, where it was tested on a pilot-plant basis starting in 1985. Marketed by SMS/Concast, the first commercial unit was ordered by Nucor late in 1986, and construction was started at Crawfordsville, Indiana, in the fall of 1987, with start-up achieved in mid-1989, when an 87m-thin slab was successfully cast. A year later, in June 1990 profitable operations were first attained.

The steelmaking section of Nucor's CSP plant consists of two Asea-supplied, Fuchs-constructed electric-arc AC furnaces with water-cooled sidewalls and roofs, oxy-fuel burners, and eccentric botton tapping. The furnaces are rated at 136 tonnes per heat and have split shells 6.7m in diameter, 61cm electrodes, and 65MVA Ferranti-Packard transformers. Tap-to-tap times are in the 90–100 min. range, and alloy additions are made automatically at the ladle or ladle-metallurgy station. The latter is served by two ladle-transfer cars utilizing a single track and has two ladle furnaces equipped with induction stirring systems and 17MVA transformers, as well as a lid-type vacuum degassing unit. Steel is tapped from the arc furnaces at 1593° C and its temperature raised to 1621° C in the ladle furnace. Some one-fifth of the steel melted is processed through the vacuum degasser. Tapped heats are 113 tonnes, leaving a 23-tonne liquid heel in the furnace after each tap.

Monitored by computer-control systems, the 113-ton covered ladle of refined steel is transported to a ladle car and positioned over the caster's 15-tonne tundish. The steel is poured via slidegate and shrouded tube into the tundish, which then directs the flow through a specially designed, submerged, ceramic nozzle into an SMS-patented, funnel-shaped casting mold. The nozzle, which permits the liquid steel to flow out of opposing sides to evenly fill the mold as a cast is started, extends some 10.2 to 12.7cm into the water-cooled copper mold, which is 76.2cm deep and forms a slab 50mm thick and 135mm wide.

The slab exits the caster at a rate more than three times that common to conventional machines, namely, at some 5.5m per minute, compared to the approximate 1.5m per minute realized in casting a 200mm thick slab, thereby permitting an equivalent throughput of about 160 tonnes per hour. Given the 50mm slab's rapid solidification, it requires containment in the caster over just 5.0m of its length, compared to 20–40m in conventional casters, and has a bending radius of just 3.0m. Special mold powders are required to help sustain these high casting speeds, which has created problems because they sometimes fuse to the slab's surface and thereafter result in surface defects in the finished hot-rolled sheets.

The thin-cast slabs, sheared to lengths of 35–43m and weighing 18,000–22,000kg, are passed into a 160m roller-hearth equalizing furnace using Stein-Huerty designs, directly linking the caster and the plant's hot-strip mill. The furnace imparts uniform slab temperatures to within 9.5° C and consumes 0.6 million BTU's per tonne versus the 2.0 million required by many slab-reheating furnaces to bring thick, inventoried slabs back to rolling temperature.

It is possible to hold the thin-cast slabs in the equalizing furnace for up to 20 minutes to accommodate the rolling mill's demands. The slabs are transferred to the mill at rolling speed for entry into the first of four, increased to five, finishing stands.

However, prior to rolling, the slabs pass through a high-pressure water descaling unit to remove scale built up in the equalizing furnace. This desealing process has been another source of difficulty in that excess scale is sometimes rolled into the sheet surface; the problem has been addressed by adding to the plant's descaling capabilities. More-complex surface problems, however, have affected about one-quarter of the coils rolled from thin-cast steels within the carbon range of 0.12 to 0.2 percent, with the finished coils displaying longitudinal folds or cracks from 7.5 to 12.5 thousandths of a cm deep.

The hot-strip mill at Nucor's CSP plant incorporates such advanced rolling techniques as automatic gauge control, hydraulic screwdowns, roll bending, and continuous variable crown control. Entry speed is 18m per minute and exit speed 365m per minute, with individual stands making reductions in excess of 50 percent. These rolling speeds are much slower than the maximums of conventional mills, which range to 1220m per minute, which sometimes results in a thicker and rougher oxide scale on the hot-rolled coils, a problem requiring adjustments in descaling and laminar cooling from the original design. Further, the high reductions lead to excess roll wear—more than twice that occurring on conventional mills—which necessitates roll changing every ten to twelve hours. This is accomplished by means of automatic roll changers in approximately twelve minutes.

The hot mill's electrical components, including 9500hp drive moters and its computer-control systems, were supplied by Westinghouse, along with spare parts and systems engineering work. As originally designed, the mill was initially able to roll finished sheets in thicknesses of 2.54 to 12.7mm, although adding a fifth rolling mill stand has permitted thinner gauges to be produced, reportedly down to a minimum of 1.7mm. Finished hot bands off the downcoiler weigh approximately 23 tonnes, and can be produced at a rate of some 907,000 tonnes annually, the plant's designed capacity, which is being expanded by 815,000 tonnes. Downstream operations encompass pickling, cold rolling, and galvanizing.

The plant's buildings contain its electric-furnace melt shop, continuous thin-slab caster, hot-strip mill through its down-coiler, and space for hot-coil storage, covering some 183,000 square meters. Nucor has another 122,000 square meters of equipment under the roof at its pickling and cold-rolling facilities, for a total of 305,000 square meters.

The hot section of Nucor's Crawfordsville plant carried an initial investment cost of approximately $200 million, with an additional $100 million in funding divided equally to cover break-in costs and working-capital requirements. Since its start-up, the hot end has received additional capital infusions to provide scale-breaking and cooling modifications and to add a fifth finishing-mill stand at a cost of $13 million. In the final analysis, therefore, actual hot-end capital costs have likely approximated $315 million or some $435 per tonne of finished hot-rolled capacity. The plant's cold section, encompassing its pickling line, using a cold-reduction mill purchased from Klockner, and a temper-rolling facility, carried a cost of $65 million, and the used galvanizing line an additional $24 million.

Operated at design capacity, the Crawfordsville plant employs 402 nonunion workers, about 300 in producing hot-rolled coil and 100 in its cold-rolling section. Specific labor inputs are 0.8 to 0.9 man-hours per tonne of hot-rolled coil and 1.4–1.5 man-hours per tonne of cold-rolled sheet. These labor requirements include production workers, as well as maintenance, administrative, and marketing personnel.

Operating crews are employed in 12-hour work shifts over a 42-hour average work week. The plant is operated on a 24-hour per day basis using four crews. Crews 1 and 2 work the day and night shifts, respectively, for four days, while crews 3 and 4 are off. Then crews 3 and 4 work days and nights, respectively, and crews 1 and 2 are off. The next week, crews 1 and 2 work three days and then have four days off, and crews 3 and 4 do the reverse. The four crews work the same 4-3-3-4 schedule over a period of 5–17 weeks, and then the day crews switch shifts with the night crews.

As to the Crawfordsville plant's scrap and other operating inputs, it is important to note that the Indiana location was selected because of its proximity to a concentration of manufacturing activity that generates considerable quantities of higher quality, prompt-industrial scrap. Nucor reports encountering few problems with physical properties in maintaining the total residual level of the plant's melt at less than 0.25 percent residuals (Cu, Ni, Cr, Mo, SN) without any detrimental effects. Still, it has been necessary to supplement the plant's electric-furnace charge with DRI, which on average has amounted to some 10 percent of the total inputs employed and is acquired mainly from Russia for $120 per tonne delivered. Nucor is presently constructing an iron carbide plant in Trinidad to produce its own supplemental electric-furnace feed.

Finished-product size, dimensions, and coil weights have already been reviewed in the course of discussing the technical characteristics of the plant's various equipment components. Regarding acceptance of the sheet steel produced, an important consideration is that Nucor is its own best customer, utilizing a significant unreported share of the plant's output to manufacture steel decking for use by its own construction subcidiary. This provides an outlet for sheet product with less-than-satisfactory quality characteristics, particularly in regard to surface imperfections. External sales of both hot- and cold-rolled sheets have been made for such noncritical applications as automobile speaker brackets, television picture-tube frames, folding chairs, children's toys, welded pipe and tubing, and various building components.

In terms of the CSP concept's development potential, Nucor assessed its Crawfordsville experience to be successful enough to construct the company's second CSP unit at Hickman, Arkansas, which incorporates a hot-strip mill with six finishing stands to permit the rolling of thinner gauge product. Finished steel output at Hickman is limited to hot-rolled coil, with an annual capacity of 1.1 million tons and a construction cost of about $300 million plus break-in and working-capital requirements. Regarding Nucor's assessment of CSP technology the following quote from the company's chairman and CEO, F. Kenneth Iverson, is most revealing: "We have no illusions. We recognize that other thin slab or net shape casting processes will be developed that will be equally or even more successful. There will be refinements and process improvements. . . . There is no ultimate process."

In-Line Strip Production (ISP). The world's second commercial plant incorporating the compact-strip approach and the first such plant in Europe was installed at Cremona, Italy, by Italian specialty-steel producer Finarvedi. The technology employed, namely, ISP for in-line strip production, evolved starting in 1987 from trials conducted at Mannesmann Steelworks in Duisburg, Germany, and from Mannesman's joint work with Arvedi in converting a standard caster for thin-slab production at Acciaieria Tubificio Arvedi, one of the Arvedi group's operating companies. Marketed by Mannesmann-Demag, the first commercial ISP plant was ordered by Arvedi in May 1989, started break-in operations toward the end of 1991, and achieved break-even results in mid-1993.

Steelmaking at Arvedi's ISP plant is accomplished in a single 100-tonne electric furnace and a similarly sized ladle-furnace facility. Molten steel is supplied to the plant's thin-slab caster via a revolving two-turret system, which supports and moves both ladles filled with steel and prepared tundishes into postion for casting. Compared to the conventional, rail-operated units, the turret system permits faster, more flexible changing of ladles and tundishes during multiple-sequence casting and is more accurate in positioning the tundish's submerged nozzle into the casting machine's mold. The nozzle is proportioned to the mold's geometry with a thickness of 30mm and a width of 250mm. It is manufactured of alumina-graphite-enriched, isostatically pressed refractory material and permits a casting rate of 3.0 tonnes per minute.

The caster's vertical, bow-type mold of special Mannesmann

design for thin-slab casting has an upper portion comprised of water-cooled copper plates with plain and parallel wide faces. This is a feature of well-proven, conventional caster molds and provides ample space for insertion of the flat-shaped submerged nozzle and also for initial solidification of the cast strand's outer shell without risking harmful deformation. The mold's vertical portion is followed tangentially by its curved portion with a radius of 5.2m, the total length of the mold being 1000m.

Within the mold, the slab, which still has a liquid core, is 650–1330mm wide by 60mm thick, and immediately upon emerging from the mold it is subjected to cast-rolling, first with a liquid core by means of twelve pairs of tapered rollers and then by sixteen pairs of multiple rollers in the caster's withdrawal section. This so-called soft reduction takes the slab's thickness down to 40mm, whereupon a further reduction is made in a solid state on a three-stand, high-reduction unit to obtain a final slab thickness of 15mm. This cast-rolling process results in a continuous reduction in slab thickness in numerous small increments, which, in addition to permitting a finished-sheet gauge as low as 1.7mm, imparts a high globular structure to the steel with little or no segregation.

After a pendulum shear separates the starter bar and cuts the thin slab to lengths, depending on the coil weights to be produced, the slabs pass through an induction-heated furnace for temperature recovery and equalization and are then coiled in a special "Cremona Box" furnace, which permits two slabs to be housed on dual mandrels, one for coiling and the other for uncoiling prior to rolling. The coil box serves as a buffer between continuous casting and hot rolling, compensating for their different operating speeds and permitting the plant's hot-strip mill to operate at optimal rolling temperatures and maximum efficiency.

The ISP hot-strip mill has four, 4-high continuous finishing stands, each equipped with hydraulic automatic gauge control, universal profile control, work-roll bending, roll shifting, and rapid roll changing. These features provide wide ranges of crown and shape control, as well as smooth roll wear, and are designed to produce a finished sheet to close gauge tolerances with excellent flatness and profile characteristics. The rolling-mill configuration at Cremona provides space for a fifth finishing stand should sheet gauge below 1.7mm be desired at some future time.

The finished sheet exits the fourth stand at the relatively low delivery speed of 600m per minute, about one-half the conventional rate, and is then cooled on the mill's laminar-flow cooling system to optimal temperature for coiling and final removal. The finished coils weigh approximately 22 tonnes, are 650–1330mm wide, and range in gauge from 1.7 to 22mm. They are capable of being produced at a rate of 500,000 annual tonnes, the ISP unit's designed capacity.

Exclusive of the Cremona plant's electric-furnace melt shop, the ISP unit, extending from the caster's two-turret ladle and tundish system through the downcoiler, is 181.3m in length, which is divided as follows: 28.4m through the high reduction unit and pendulum shear for thin slabs, 38.4m through the equalizing furnace and Cremona Box, 31.5m through the fourth finishing stand, and 83.0m through the laminar-cooling system and downcoiler.

Final manning tables and capital-cost breakdowns for Arvedi's ISP plant have not been made available and could not be considered typical because it is the first such plant ever constructed. It is estimated, however, that staffing involves two to three hundred workers, including maintenance workers, and that subsequent plants replicating the facilities at Cremona will require a total capital investment of $250 to $300 million, including provision for break-in and working-capital needs. This represents $500–$600 per annual tonne of finished hot-rolled sheet capacity.

The sheet grades to be rolled by Arvedi encompass both low-grade and high-grade carbon steel, as well as stainless austenitic and ferretic steel. Particularly when carbon grades are produced, supplementary charges of DRI are required to lower the residual levels that would otherwise be imparted to the melt by exclusively using scrap. It is significant that two ISP units presently under consideration by the Turkish steelmaker Cukurova are being planned with BOF rather than electric-furnace steelmaking support.

VAI's Conroll Process. Voest-Alpine Industrienlagenbau of Austria inaugurated a research and engineering program into thin-slab casting in the early 1980s. Its findings provided the basis for a commercial plant producing stainless steel in cooperation with Avesta AB of Sweden, which continuously cast its first thin slabs 80mm thick and 1560mm wide in December 1988. The first thin-slab caster for stainless steel, Avesta's facility involved the revamping of an existing conventional caster. This operating experience and further investigation at Avesta led VAI to institute casting and rolling campaigns using its technology to produce carbon steel at Voest-Alpine Stahl in Linz, Austria. Based on the success of its work at Linz, VAI initiated marketing of its "Conroll" process early in 1991.

Starting with a butterfly ladle turret, a Conroll unit introduces either BOF or electric-furnace steel into a 22-tonne caster tundish, which employs a submerged-entry nozzle to fill a straight, parallel mold having copper plates that incorporate inverse water cooling to ensure a uniform slab temperature. The cast strand has a bow radius of 3m, moves through the caster at a maximum speed of 4m per minute or at an average casting rate of 2.5 tonnes per minute, and has as-cast dimensions of 70mm thick and 800–1600mm wide. The submerged-entry nozzle linking the tundish and the mold permits a wide range of casting speeds, and a mold-level control system holds the meniscus within a close tolerance independent of the casting speed employed. The strand is guided through the caster by small, intermittent rollers, and slab bending and straightening occur with minimum interface strain at the liquid–solid interphase.

Upon exiting the caster, the thin 70mm slab has a uniform temperature and is cut to specified lengths by hydraulic shears, prior to entering a roller-hearth furnace, an essential buffer between Conroll's caster and rolling mill. The furnace, which heats and equalizes the slab's temperature, varies in length depending upon the specific coil weight required, while the length of the buffer period required varies with the casting speed employed.

The heated thin slabs, having a maximum temperature of 1150° C, are passed through a high-pressure water descaler and rolled on a continuous hot-strip mill with six finishing stands, considered appropriate for producing finished sheets in a thickness range of 1.7–12mm. The stands are equipped with modern rolling technology, including hydraulic screwdowns, roll bending and shifting, and automatic controls for sheet profile, thickness, and flatness. Exiting the sixth stand, the hot strip is subjected to laminar-flow cooling and is then gathered on the mill's downcoiler.

VAI has most frequently presented Conroll as a medium-capacity plant concept, incorporating twin continuous-casting strands linked to a single rolling mill, which provides a maximum designed annual capacity of 1.6 million tonnes of finished hot-rolled coils. The plant is designed to produce a variety of carbon-steel grades, and at full production has a manpower requirement totaling 212 workers, including those engaged in maintenance. A capital-cost determination awaits construction of the first commercial unit for carbon-steel output and will vary depending upon the design parameters selected.

Thin-Slab Conticaster (TSC). Danieli Group, the Italian mill builder, has applied its engineering and design capabilities to develop a compact-strip production technique it calls TSC, for thin-slab conticaster. Actually, Danieli's design encompasses more than just continuous casting, for it directly links electric-arc steelmaking, thin-slab casting, and hot-strip rolling in an in-line arrangement targeted to produce 600,000 to 650,000 tonnes per year of finished hot-rolled coils.

TSC is designed to employ a single 120-tonne electric-arc steelmaking furnace to melt scrap or varying combinations of scrap and DRI, depending on the steel grades to be produced. The recommended furnace employs oxy-fuel burners and eccentric bottom tapping, and is capable of tap-to-tap times averaging 70 minutes. It is intended to serve primarily as a melter and to operate in conjunction with a secondary-refining unit, either a ladle furnace, a vacuum oxygen decarburation (VOD) unit, or an argon oxygen decarburation (AOD) unit, according to the grades and qualities of steel required. Shrouding protects the steel from reoxidation during transfer from the ladle to the continuous-casting tundish.

The thin-slab conticaster itself is a single-strand unit with a submerged nozzle and with a vertical curved mold, 1200mm in length, and designed to cast slabs 50–75mm thick and 1000–1650mm wide at speeds of 2–5m per minute. Exiting the machine, the cast thin slabs are cut by oxygen torches or flying shear. In the as-cast state, the slabs have a temperature of 950° C, which is then raised prior to rolling 1,150° C in an "equalization" furnace. The Danieli-designed walking-beam furnace is fitted with inlet and outlet roller tables linking it directly to the conticaster and hot rolling mill, respectively. The furnace makes it possible to store slabs in case of downstream problems at the rolling mill.

TSC's hot-strip mill employs six finishing stands equipped with such rolling advances as hydraulic screwdowns, roll bending, and roll shifting. It is designed to produce finished hot-rolled sheets in gauges of 2.0–12.7mm and in widths up to 1600mm. Maximum coil weights off the mill's downcoiler approach 30 tonnes and the plant's finished-product capacity is designed at the aforementioned maximum of 650,000 tonnes. The plant's labor requirements are estimated at 2.5 man-hours per tonne.

Krupp's ECCO Mill. Germany's Krupp Industrietechnik has devised a compact-strip technique based on using a single-stand Platzer high-reduction mill to roll an 80mm slab into finished hot-rolled sheet with a minimum gauge of 1.8mm. Called an ECCO mill, combining "economic" and "compact," the approach evolved from Krupp's experience in rolling-mill construction over many years. The focal element in Krupp's design is the Platzer mill for achieving thickness reductions of up to 98 percent in a single pass, thereby providing a rolling alternative suited to compact-mill operations.

The linked elements in Krupp's ECCO unit are a curved-mold slab caster equipped with ladle turret, tundish, and straightening unit that supplies slabs to the Platzer rolling mill at uniform temperature via an equalizing furnace and a single set of feed rolls, which make an initial 10–20 percent reduction in the slab. The Platzer mill then makes its 98 percent reduction.

As to the Platzer mill's design, it comprises two stationary back-up beams, around which two rings of work rolls rotate in direction with intermediate backup rolls. The work rolls and the backup rolls can be moved radially in the driven cages, run synchronously in counterrotation to one another, and rotate in planetary motion around the backup beam. The feed rolls slowly feed the slabs into the roll gap in the high-reduction mill stand. At this point, each twenty-four pairs of work rolls, which rotate at high speeds, rolls a thin layer of material from both sides of the slab until the finished strip is obtained. In a sense, it is as if the slab were rolled on a twenty-four-stand rolling mill, with very small reductions being performed at each stand, the result being a sheet with a very uniform macrostructure and good material properties.

Krupp's ECCO mill design provides for finished sheet capacities ranging from 300,000 to 750,000 tonnes, depending principally on casting speeds, which can vary from 1.4–3.6m per minute. Although the approach has been examined by a number of steel companies, its implementation has thus far been limited to a 40cm pilot mill operated by Krupp in Germany. Projected costs for a 300,000-tonne unit ranging from $150–$170 million have also been a deterrent, although the single-stand feature has a definite attraction to minimill operators. Other single-stand alternatives, most notably the Sendzimir mill, are also being examined.

Thyssen's CPR Process. Thyssen Stahl of Germany has been experimenting with its own compact-strip technique and has constructed a pilot plant at Duisburg in a joint venture with Usinor and SMS to test a thin-slab caster capable of producing slabs 22mm thick and under. The caster design employed by Thyssen is somewhat comparable to that of Mannessmann/Arvedi in that the slab emerges from the caster mold at 50mm thickness and is immediately reduced with a liquid core while still in the casting machine. However, Thyssen's design objectives call for rolling the slabs on only one or two four-high rolling mill stands to significantly reduce capital costs.

Called the CPR process (for casting-pressing-rolling), Thyssen's technique has achieved good results in test rolling its thin slabs on a conventional hot-strip mill into hot coils with a sheet thickness of 4–10mm, a width of 1,200mm, and a weight of 15 tons. Encouraged by the results, Thyssen is considering an investment in a 600,000-annual-tonne commercial plant, which could be ready as early as 1996. At the same time, the company continues to experiment with a "double-roller" process for casting steel strips 1.5–8mm thick and has achieved promising results at a pilot line located in France, the objective being to produce stainless and electrical sheets.

Tippins's TSP Process. U.S. mill builder Tippins Inc., a world leader in Steckel-mill technology, has developed a compact-strip technique called TSP (for "Tippins Strip Process"). The technique combines a thin-slab caster for intermediate thickness slabs of 100mm and a single-stand Steckel rolling mill to produce between 400,000 and 1.2 million tonnes of finished hot strip in gauges ranging from 1.5 to 20mm and in widths up to 2,500mm. This is considerably wider than the maximums attainable using thinner slabs, and TSP's use of an intermediate slab also seeks to avoid the surface difficulties other thin-slab casters have encountered. A standard TSP plant with a capacity of up to 1.2 million annual tonnes carries an estimated capital cost under $200 million, covering an electric-furnace steelmaking shop, continuous caster, equalizing furnace, and Steckel rolling mill.

The steelmaking shop can utilize an AC or DC electric furnace or basic-oxygen units linked to a ladle-metallurgy station to deliver steel to the caster in 100 to 150 tonne heats. The thin-slab caster is a single-strand, low-head unit that forms 100mm intermediate slabs at 2.5 meters per minute in maximum lengths of 22 meters. The slabs pass directly into a walking-hearth equalizing and reheat furnace 24 meters wide and 20 meters long, capable of processing 275 tonnes of cast slabs per hour.

The focal point of the TSP process is a single-stand Steckel mill with dual coiling furnaces, one located at each end of the mill, that retain rolling temperatures and permit the one stand to perform the required function. The mill is a four-high reversing rougher and finishing unit and is equipped with automatic gauge control, roll bending, and optional roll shifting. The mill incorporates a vertical edger for width control, a high-pressure descaling system, laminar-flow cooling, an upcoiler, and full Level I and Level II process controls. While TSP direct charges its normalized slabs to the Steckel mill, the continuous caster and mill can be operated independently to minimize yield losses should either unit be taken out of service.

TSP has not been subjected to experimental or pilot-plant testing. However, unlike other compact-strip approaches utilizing heretofore untried technologies for casting and rolling thinner slabs, the TSP design incorporates already-proven facilities at each of its operating stages. Its relatively low capital cost, estimated at about half that of alternative compact-strip techniques, could make flat-rolled production accessible to a wider segment of the minimill population.

Finishing Operations

As near-net-shape casting becomes more widely applied to form not only thin slabs, but also beam blanks, other shapes, and eventually sheets, less downstream mechanical working will be required to obtain finished-product dimensions. This means that rolling technology and operating practices will have to be adapted to impart desirable mechanical properties to the finished product despite fewer working hours. Because molten steel cools and solidifies more rapidly when thinner shapes are cast, final worked products will have a more nearly amorphous structure than if rolled from conventionally cast thick shapes.

A number of ongoing changes in rolling technology will continue to be directed at maintaining and optimizing process heat in the interest of energy conservation and operating efficiency. Direct rolling of semifinished shapes after continuous casting—also referred to as "hot charging"—eliminates reheating requirements, reduces semifinished steel inventories, and improves overall process yields by avoiding scale losses that would otherwise evolve in cooling and reheating the semifinished sections. Energy savings also result from utilizing a coil box in hot-strip rolling to maintain more uniform heat within the steel by lessening its atmospheric exposure. By limiting heat loss, a coil box permits existing hot-strip mills to roll larger coils and can also reduce the required number of finishing stands. Atmospheric exposure can also be limited by thermal shielding of the hot-strip line leading to the finishing train, in some cases incorporating heating elements into the enclosure.

Other advances in finishing technology likely to find wider use include the six-high cold mill to improve the quality of cold-rolled sheets, low-temperature rolling to conserve energy and impart extra strength to plate and strip products, and in-line sizing mills positioned between the continuous caster and rolling mill to maximize caster throughput and minimize semifinished inventories.

A very recent entry into the thin-slab rolling mill combination is SMS and Sendzimir. SMS will link the Sendzimir planetary rolling mill with its thin-slab caster. The Sendzimir mill will reduce the slab in one pass.

6
Summary

The world steel industry at the present time is a study in contrasts. Overall, considering the production of the entire world, there has been very little growth in the past decade. In 1982 total production was 645 million tonnes, and in 1992 it was 714 million tonnes. Contrast these figures with the growth that took place between 1966 and 1976: in 1966 total world production was 473 million tonnes, but by 1976 world production was 685 million tonnes. In the developing countries, however, steel has had a remarkable growth between 1980, when it was 102 million tonnes, and 1992, when production reached 214 million tonnes. Meanwhile, production in the industrialized countries declined from 406 million tonnes in 1980 to 359 million tonnes in 1992.

In terms of exports, the developing countries accounted for 9.5 million tonnes in 1980 and for 27 million tonnes in 1991, whereas the industrialized countries accounted for 111 million tonnes in 1980 and for 123 million tonnes in 1991.

Growth has been substantial in the developing countries, particularly in the People's Republic of China, South Korea, and Brazil, while in the industrialized countries only three countries—Canada, Italy, and Spain—have equaled their production figures of 1974 in subsequent years.

In the years ahead the industrialized countries will probably shrink in size by as much as 10 percent in total crude steel production, whereas the developing countries will grow by probably 25 percent. The People's Republic of China plans to increase its output to 100 million tonnes from the current 89 million tonnes by the year 2000. Other developing countries also have ambitious plans. This projected growth on the part of the developing countries and a relatively small shrinkage on the part of the industrialized countries means that competition betwen the two will increase considerably, particularly as the developing countries reach out for export markets on a worldwide basis. Competition between the two worlds, the developing world and the industrialized world, will have an effect on total world steel production in terms of where it will be produced and how much will be produced in the various areas.

Another major contrast in the steel industry is the growth of the minimill versus the stagnation of integrated steel plants. The integrated plants in the industrialized countries will probably not increase in number for the remainder of this decade. This is in keeping with the slight decline in total steel production that is foreseen for this area of the world. Whatever increase there will be in the industrialized countries will be in the minimill segment, particularly as the minimills strive to produce flat-rolled products and heavy structural sections.

The developing countries will build a number of new integrated plants. This is particularly true for China, India, and Taiwan. In other developing countries, such as South Korea and Brazil, there will be an increase in minimills rather than a growth in the number of integrated steel plants.

As the decade moves on, more steel will be made by the electric-furnace method. Currently, there is a tendency to shift from the blast furnace/BOF combination to the electric furnace to produce steel. This trend is developing in the industrialized countries. An example is Arbed in Luxembourg, which is substituting electric furnaces for basic-oxygen converters and blast furnaces.

The increase in electric-furnace output, which could rise to as much as 40–45 percent of total world steel production by the year 2000, will require an increase in direct-reduced iron (DRI) and iron carbide in order to supplement the scrap charge commonly used in electric furnaces. This is particularly true of the minimills and other electric-furnace operations that will be producing sheets, since it is difficult, if not impossible, to produce deep-drawing quality sheets with steel made from a 100 percent scrap charge. Iron carbide and DRI will have to be added to dilute some of the tramp elements that are found even in the best scrap.

By 2000, there will be a number of electric-furnace mills producing sheets. Perhaps as much as 10–15 percent of the sheet production on a worldwide basis will be produced from electric furnaces.

Competition, particularly in the lower grades of sheet production, will become more severe as additional minimills are put into operation to produce these sheets. However, there will be a large portion of steel sheets, particularly of the higher quality, produced by the blast-furnace/BOF combination.

In regard to substitute materials, competition, particularly from aluminum and plastics, will become more severe as the 1990s progress. The aluminum and plastics manufacturers are striving to widen their participation in the automotive and appliance markets, as well as others. Their success in this respect has been somewhat limited, although much publicity has been given to the advances they have made. Steel is still by far the most important material used in the production of automobiles and in construction. This will remain true through the end of the present decade.

In terms of basic steel mill facilities, such as coke ovens, blast furnaces, and basic-oxygen converters, which are found principally in industrialized countries, there will be a tendency to reduce these units in favor of lower-capital-investment facilities, such as the electric furnace. Further, since coke ovens are responsible for a significant degree of pollution, by reducing their number, this will be greatly reduced.

In the industrialized world, few blast-furnaces will be built in the remainder of the 1990s. Difficult decisions will have to be made when blast furnaces are due for relining. A large blast furnace producing 10,000 tons a day requires approximately $100 million for a reline. Such a large investment must be considered very carefully before a commitment is made. There are other means of producing iron, such as the DIOS and Corex processes, which could well be installed in place of a relined blast furnace. The developing countries however, will tend to build blast furnaces in order to expand their steelmaking capacity. This will be particularly true in China, India, and Taiwan.

One of the recent developments in technology has been the injection of powdered coal into the blast furnaces to partially replace coke. As much as 400 pounds per tonne of iron has been injected, thus reducing the coke rate by at least 40 percent. This practice is widespread in Europe and Japan, but in the United States it is just beginning to take hold. During the next few years most of the blast furnaces in the United States, and for that matter those throughout the industrialized world, will be using coal injection to reduce the coke rate, and as a consequence will reduce the pollution associated with coke ovens.

Notes

1. *Japan Economic Journal,* 4 August, 1981, p. 6.
2. *American Metal Market* 27 July, 1993, p. 4.
3. *Groves Report, Metal Bulletin,* 21, 22, 27 April 1993, 6 May, 1993.
4. From a speech given by Wang Gong Cheng at the Iron Ore and Steel: Tapping Into the Pacific Rim Conference, Sydney, Australia, May 11, 1993.
5. Sources: (1) A speech given by Steve Lee, Assistant to the President of China Steel at the Steel Survival Strategies VIII, 1993. (2) Metal Bulletin, July 22, 1993. (3) Reuters News Service, July 10, 1993.
6. J. R. Miller *Iron and Steelmaker,* May 1984, p. 20.
7. *American Metal Market,* 23 December, 1986, p. 3.
8. John Correnti, *"Mini-Mills: The Moment of Truth"* Conference in Milan, Italy, 14 May 1993.
9. *American Metal Market,* 24 May 1993, p. 37.
10. *33 Metal Producing,* October 1995, p. 46.
11. Peter F. Marcus and Karlis M. Kirsis, *"Steel: Who are the Winners in the 1990s?,"* presentation to Steel Survival Strategies VIII Conference, New York City, 22 June, 1993, p. 32.
12. David H. Hoag, *"Are the Major Mills Competitive with Minimills in the Flat Rolled Steel Business,"* presentation to Steel Survival Strategies VIII Conference, New York City, 22 June 1993, p. 4.
13. Manager, Industry Marketing, Automotive, United States Steel Corporation.
14. Descriptive material provided by Midrex Direct Reduction Corporation.
15. Process descriptions derived largely from company sources.

Bibliography

American Iron and Steel Institute, *Annual Statistical Report*. Washington, D.C.: AISI, various years.

———. *Directory of Iron and Steel Works of the United States and Canada*. Washington, D.C.: AISI, various years.

American Metal Market. New York: Capital Cities/ABC Inc. Diversified Publishing Group, various daily issues.

American Metal Market Co. *Metal Statistics: The Purchasing Guide of the Metal Industries*. New York: American Metal Market, various years.

Berry, Bryan. "Hot Band at 0.66 Manhours Per Ton," *New Steel* (October, 1993): 20–26.

British Steel Corporation, Statistical Services. *International Steel Statistics: World Tables*. Croydon, England: BSC, various years.

Concast, AG. *World Survey of Continuous Casting Machines for Steel*. Zurich, Switzerland: Concast Documentation Center, various annual editions.

Corrent, John. "Mini-Mills: The Moment of Truth," *International Minimill Conference*. Milan, Italy: May 14, 1993.

Eisenstein, Paul A. "Recycling Autos Is Harder As Carmakers Use More Plastic," *Investor's Daily* (October 25, 1990): 21.

Ess, T.J. *The Hot Strip Mill Generation II*. Pittsburgh; Association of Iron and Steel Engineers, 1970.

Etienne, Gilbert; Astier, Jacques; Bhushan, Hari; and Zhong, Dai. *Asian Crucible: The Steel Industry in China and India*. Geneva, Switzerland: Modern Asia Research Center, 1990.

European Coal and Steel Community. *Investments in the Community Coalmining and Iron and Steel Industries*. Luxembourg: ECSC, surveys of various years.

Fruehan, R.J. "Challenges and Opportunities in the Steel Industry," *Iron & Steelmaker* (March, 1993): 59–64.

Fukushima, Tsutomu. "Smelting Reduction in Japan," *Future Iron-making Processes & Procedures*. Hamilton, Ontario, Canada, June 14–15, 1990.

Hicks, Jonathan. "An Industrial Comeback Story: U.S. is Competing Again in Steel," *The New York Times* (March 31, 1992): 1.

Hoag, David H. "Are the Major Mills Competitive with Minimills in the Flat Rolled Steel Business," *Steel Survival Strategies VIII Conference*. New York: June 22, 1993.

Hogan, William T. *Capital Investment in Steel: A World Plan for the 1990's*. New York: Lexington Books, 1992.

———. *Economic History of the Iron and Steel Industry in the United States*, five volumes. Lexington, Massachusetts: Lexington Books, 1971.

———. "Future Steel Plans in the Third World" *Iron and Steel Engineer 54* (November, 1977): 25–37.

———. *Minimills and Integrated Mills: A Comparison of Steelmaking in the United States*. Lexington, Massachusetts: Lexington Books, 1987.

———. *Siderurgia Mundial: Perspectives para la Decada del '80*. Buenos Aires, Argentina: Centro Internacional de Informacion Empresaria, 1981.

———. "The Future World Crisis in Coke," *Iron and Steel Engineer* (December, 1992): 32–35.

———. *The 1970's: Critical Years for Steel*. Lexington, Massachusetts: Lexington Books, 1972.

———. *World Steel in the 1980s: A Case of Survival*. Lexington, Massachusetts: Lexington Books, 1983.

Hogan, William T., and Koelble, Frank T. *Analysis of the U.S. Metallurgical Coke Industry*. Washington, D.C.: U.S. Department of Commerce, 1979.

———. *Direct Reduction as an Ironmaking Alternative in the United States*. Washington, D.C.: U.S. Department of Commerce, 1981.

———. "Economics of Ladle Refining," *Steel Technology International* (1989): 177–180.

Holschuh, Lenard J. "Report of the Secretary General," *International Iron and Steel Institute Twenty-Seventh Annual Meetings and Conference*. Paris, France: October 3, 1993.

Huskonen, Wallace D. "Italian Mini-Mill Designed for Quality, Flexibility," *33 Metal Producing* (October, 1993): 42–46.

Innace, Joseph J. and Dress, Abby. *Igniting Steel: Korea's POSCO Lights the Way*. Huntington, New York: Global Village Press, 1992.

Instituto Brasileiro de Siderurgica. *IBS Yearbook, Anuario Estatistico da Industria Siderurgica Brasilerira*. Brazil: IBS, various years.

International Iron and Steel Institute, Committee on Statistics. *Steel Statistical Yearbook*. Brussels: IISI, various years.

———. *Steel Statistics of Developing Countries*. Brussels, Belgium: IISI, various editions.

Iron and Steel Engineer. Pittsburgh, Pennsylvania: Association of Iron and Steel Engineers, various issues.

Isenberg-O'Loughlin, Jo. "Breaking the Mold," *33 Metal Producing* (October, 1993): 22–30 and 58.

———. "DC Arcs Strike Again," *33 Metal Producing* (November, 1993): 18–21 and 49–50.

Japan Economic Journal. Tokyo, Japan: Nikon Keizai Shimbun, Inc., various weekly issues.

Japan Iron & Steel Federation. *The Steel Industry of Japan.* Tokyo: JISF, various years.

King, James F. *World Capacity and Production Report: Finished Steel Flat and Coated Products.* Newcastle upon Tyne: James F. King, May, 1993.

Kingori, W. "Aluminum in Automaking: Its Time Has Come," *Iron & Steelmaker* (August, 1993): 15–17.

Koelble, Frank T. "Strategies for Restructuring the U.S. Steel Industry." *33 Metal Producing.* Vol. 24, No. 12 (December, 1986): 28–33.

Marcus, Peter F. and Kirsis, Karlis M. "Steel: Who are the Winners in the 1990's," *Steel Survival Strategies VIII Conference.* New York: June 22, 1993.

McAloon, T.P. "Steel-Back in the Driver's Seat," *Iron & Steelmaker* (August, 1993) 23–25.

McManus, George J. "Georgetown Steel Blazes the Trail of Direct Reduced Iron," *New Steel* (October, 1993): 28–30.

Metal Bulletin. London, England: Metal Bulletin Journals Ltd., various issues.

Metal Bulletin Monthly. London, England: Metal Bulletin Journals Ltd., various issues.

Midrex Corporation. *Direct from Midrex.* Charlotte, North Carolina: Midrex, various quarterly issues.

Miller, J.R. "Giant Minimill Companies," *Iron and Steelmaker* (May, 1984): 20–26.

Motor Vehicle Manufacturers Association. *Motor Vehicle Facts and Figures.* Detroit, Michigan: MVMA, various years.

———. *World Motor Vehicle Data.* Detroit, Michigan: MVMA, various years.

Moore, C. and Marshall, R.I. *Steelmaking.* London: The Institute of Metals, 1991.

Organization of Economic Cooperation and Development. *The Iron and Steel Industry.* Paris, France: OECD, various years.

Peterson, Peter T. "Introduction to Advanced Steel Design: Downweighting the Automobile," *International Iron and Steel Institute Twenty-Seventh Annual Meetings and Conference.* Paris, France: October 4, 1993.

Pollock, B.A. "Plastics—Better Than Ever," *Iron & Steelmaker* (August, 1993): 19–22.

Preston, Richard. *American Steel.* New York: Prentice Hall Press, 1991.

Serjeantson, Richard; Cordero, Raymond; and Field, Andrew, eds. *Iron and Steelworks of the World*, 10th Edition. Surrey, England: Metal Bulletin Books, Ltd., 1991.

Steel Times International. Surrey, England: FMJ International Publications, Ltd., various monthly issues.

U.K. Iron and Steel Statistics Bureau. *International Steel Statistics.* Croydon, England, various countries and years.

United Nations, Economic Commission for Europe. *Quarterly Bulletin of Steel Statistics for Europe.* New York: United Nations, various years.

———. *Statistics of World Trade in Steel.* New York: United Nations, various years.

———. *The Steel Market.* New York: United Nations, various years.

United Nations, Industrial Development Organization. *Proceedings of the Second General Conference.* Lima, Peru: UNIDO, 1975.

U.S. International Trade Commission. *Steel Industry Annual Report.* Washington, D.C.: USITC, 1985–1991.

Voest-Alpine, *Co-Generation with Corex*, Linz/Dusseldorf: Voest-Alpine, 1991.

Wrigley, Al. "Ford Ditches Steel for Plastic in Body Parts," *American Metal Market* (September 17, 1990): 1 and 16.

Index

Acciaieria Tubificio Arvedi, 173
Acciai Speciali Terni, 36
Acme, 81, 105
Africa, drop in EC exports to, 72
AHMSA (Altos Hornos de Mexico), 69, 150
AHV, 81
Air Products, 22
AK Steel, 22
Allegheny-Ludlum, 106
Allied Steel and Wire, 29
Alloys, 160, 166
Alpha Steel, 29–30
Alternating-current (AC) furnaces, displacing, 158
Aluminum, use of, 5, 18, 121–28, 133–34, 185
Amalgamated Steel Mills (ASM), 65
American Iron and Steel Institute (AISI), 98, 131, 132, 155–56
American Steel and Wire Corporation, 24–25
Andrew Estates South Project, 132
An Feng Steel Company, 62
Anshan Iron and Steel Company, 40, 47
Appliance industry, 120, 135–37
Arbed, 34–35, 184
Argentina, steel industry in, 8, 11, 12, 68–69
Armco Inc., 22, 26, 81, 105, 106
Arvedi, 79, 81, 84, 117, 118, 163, 165, 167, 173–76
Atlantic, 75
Australia, steel industry in, 38–40
Automation, 141
Automotive industry, steel vs. substitute materials in, 5–6, 93, 120–28

Auto/Steel Partnership Program, 123, 124
Avesta AB of Sweden, 81, 117, 176
Avesta Sheffield, 79

Bahindcan, 46
Bangkok Steel Industry, 65
Baoshan Steel Works, 45, 46
Basic-oxygen furnaces (BOF) steel-making, 142, 143, 157, 160
Batch-type production, 139, 141
Bei Hai project, 46
Belarus, 37
Belgium, steel industry in, 9, 149
Beta Steel, 27, 30, 106, 109
Bethlehem Steel Corporation, 18, 21, 23, 105, 145
Bhushan Steel and Strip Company, 52
Birmingham Steel, 24–25, 89, 110
Black plate, 133
Blast-furnaces, 142, 145, 185–86. See also Raw materials preparation
Brastubo, 58–59
Brazil, steel industry in, 8, 11–12, 56–61
British Steel Corporation, 28–29, 129, 134, 148
Broken Hill Proprietary (BHP) of Australia, 25, 38–39, 84

California Steel Company, 26–27, 46, 106
Canada, steel industry in, 8, 9
CAP (Chilean steel group), 69
Capital costs and expenditures
  for Arvedi's ISP plant, 175
  in Australia, 38–39
  in Brazil, 56–61
  in coke-oven facilities, 145–48

for compact-strip vs. conventional production, 162–63, 167
for ECCO mill, 179
in France, 34
in Germany, 30–33
in India, 51–56
in Japan, 15–17
in Luxembourg, 35
for Nucor's CSP plant, 171
in Southeast Asia, 63–68
in Taiwan, 61–63
in U.K., 28–29
in U.S., 18–19
   integrated companies, 20–23
   by minimills, 24–28
Ceramics, 5
CF&I, 25
Chapparel, 5, 79
Chicago World's Fair (1933), 131
China Steel, 61–62, 65
Chrysler, 124, 125
Clean Air Act amendments (1990), 145, 146
Clean steel revolution, ladle refining and, 159–61
Cleveland Electric Company, 22
Clough Engineering, 39
Coal Mining Research Center of Japan, 156
Coil box in hot-strip rolling, utilizing, 182
Coke, supply of, 152–53
Coke-making operations and facilities, 144–53, 185
Compact-strip production techniques, 161–81
   concepts versus reality of, 163–65
   conventional hot-strip mills vs., 161–63
   leading concepts, 162
      compact-strip production (CSP), 163, 168–73
      in-line strip production (ISP), 163, 164, 165, 173–76
      Krupp's ECCO mill, 178–79
      thin-slab conticaster (TSC), 177–78
      Thyssen's CPR process, 164, 165, 180
      Tippin's TSP process, 180–81
      VAI's Conroll process, 176–77
   outlook for, 166–67

quality considerations with, 165–66, 167
Competition. *See also* Substitute materials
   forces reshaping steel industry, 4–6
   between industrialized and developing countries, 4, 8–12, 184
   in lower grades of sheet production, 185
   minimills and, 5, 90–92, 109–15
Computer-aided design (CAD) and manufacturing (CAM) techniques, 93
Computer-based systems, 93, 139, 141
Conners, 75
Conroll process, 176–77
Consteel process, 157–58
Construction industry, 120, 128–33
Consumers, steel, 3
   appliance industry, 120, 135–37
   automotive industry, 5–6, 93, 120–28
   construction industry, 120, 128–33
   container industry, 130, 133–35
Container industry, 130, 133–35
Continuous casting, 3, 20, 80
   ladle refining and, 159–61
   minimills and exploitation of, 74–75, 76, 81
Continuous operations, increase in, 139–41
Corex process, use of, 21–22, 42, 52, 62, 68, 154–55, 186
Correnti, John, 84
Cosinor, 59
Cosipa, 58–59
CoSteel-Dofasco, 85, 110–11
CoSteel of Canada, 29
Cost trends. *See also* Capital costs and expenditures
   integrated mill vs. minimill, 113–15
   ladle refining and, 159–60
CPR process (casting-pressing-rolling), 164, 165, 180
CRA Ltd., 155
CSN, 59
Cukurova Celik Endustrisi, 118, 176
Customer base, internationalization of U.S. industry's, 95
CVRD, 26, 57, 58, 59, 60, 69

Dae Han Steel, 42
Daiwa Steel Company, 119
Danieli Group, 110, 177–78
Decline, steel industry, 7–14, 71–73.
    See also Industrialized coun-
    tries, steel industry in
Demand, U.S. steel, 98–106
Denro Ispat Ltd., 56
Det Danske Stalvalsevaerk (DDS),
    157
Dev, Santosh Mohan, 48
Developing countries, v, 1, 4. *See also*
    Specific countries
  attitudes toward steel industry in,
    71
  blast furnaces built in, 186
  growth in production, 183
  steel industry trends in, 7–12,
    71–73
  steel production by 2000 in, 3–4
Direct-current (DC) furnaces, displac-
    ing AC furnaces with, 158
Direct-hot-charge complex (DHCC),
    114–15
Direct Iron Ore Smelting (DIOS)
    Project, 150–51, 155, 156,
    186
Direct-reduced iron (DRI), 26, 53–56,
    62, 83, 142–43, 153–54, 166,
    172, 185
Direct rolling of semifinished shapes,
    182
Direct Steelmaking Project, 155–56
Dofasco, 81
Dollar, value of, 95, 96
"Double-roller" process, 180
Dry quenching, 147, 148
Duferco Trading Company, 64

Eastern Europe, EC exports to, 72
ECCO mill, 178–79
Egypt, steel industry in, 69, 70
EKO Steel (Ekostahl), 32–33, 36, 118
Electric-furnace steelmaking, 142. *See*
    also Compact-strip production
    techniques; Minimills
  improvements in, 75–76, 157–58
  problem with, 166
  tendency to shift to, 184–85
  U.S., capacity for, 105
Electrode savings, 158
Empire Steel, 22

Employment in steel industry, 8, 9,
    171
Energy conservation, 143, 182
Energy Optimizing Furnace (EOF),
    158
England. *See* United Kingdom, steel
    industry in
Ensidesa, 150
Environmental regulations, 145–47
Eregli Demir ve Celik Fabrikalari, 37,
    118
ESSAR Gujarat, 51
European Community (EC), steel in-
    dustry in, 2, 28–38, 71–72
  drop in exports, 71–72
  France, 9, 33–34, 148–49
  Germany, 9, 30–33, 117, 147–48
  High Commission for, 13, 28, 116,
    117
  Italy, 8, 9, 35–36, 76, 77, 79, 81,
    84, 149
  Luxembourg, 34–35
  production and capacity (1980–
    1992), 12, 13–14
  raw materials preparation in,
    147–50
  reduction of capacity in, 28, 34,
    116, 117
  Russia and Ukraine, 37–38
  thin-slab casting in, 116–18
  Turkey, 8, 36–37, 118
  United Kingdom, 9, 28–30, 129
Exchange rates, 90
Exports and exports market, 9–12,
    36, 71–72, 97, 183

Falck of Italy, 39
Far East Iron Works, 65
Fastmet, 153–54
Finarvedi, 173
Finishing operations, 140, 181–82
Flat-rolled products, 5. *See also* Mini-
    mills
  defined, 98
  demand for, 98–106
    through 2010, 98–101
    supply vs., 101–6
  increased competition in, 90–92
  Japanese, 16–17
  segments of market for, 106–9
  thin-slab casting and, 79–85
Ford Motor Company, 88, 124, 125

France, steel industry in, 9, 33–34, 148–49
Frigidaire, 136
Fuch Systemtechnik shaft furnace, 157–58

General Motors, 124, 125
Geneva Steel, 81, 88
Gerdau Group, 59, 61
Germany, steel industry in, 9, 30–33, 117, 147–48
Great Britain. *See* United Kingdom, steel industry in
Grossman, Jurgen, 31–32
Growth, steel industry, 7–14, 71–73. *See also* Developing countries
Gulf States, 88
Gunawan Group, 67

Hai Kwang Enterprise, 63
Hammersley Iron PTY, 45
Hanbo Steel, 41, 47
High-end hot-strip mills, 107
HIsmelt process for direct-iron-ore smelting, 155
Holistic approach to automobile design, 125
Hoogovens, 81, 134, 148, 149
"Hot charging," 182
Hot-strip mills, 98–109. *See also* Flat-rolled products
    coil box in hot-strip rolling, using, 182
    "compact"-strip approach vs. conventional, 161–63
    European capacity, 116
    ISP, 174–75
    at Nucor's CSP plant, 170
    segments of market, 106–9
    TSC's, 178
    U.S., 101–6

ILAFA, 60
Ilva (formerly Italsider), 36, 57, 58, 148, 149
Ilva Laminata Piani, 36
Imports into U.S., 96, 97
Inchon Steel, 41–42
India, steel industry in, 8, 17, 48–56, 72, 73
Indonesia, steel industry in, 17, 63, 67–68

Industrialized countries, steel industry in, v, 1, 4. *See also* European Community (EC), steel industry in; Japan; United States, steel industry in
    attitudes toward, 71
    trends in, 4, 7–14, 71–73, 183–84
Inland Steel, 22–23, 105, 145, 147
In-line sizing mill, 182
In-line strip production (ISP), 163, 164, 165, 173–76
Integrated steel mills, 4–5
    in Brazil, 56–59
    in China, 45–47
    conventional hot-strip mill, 161–63
    in Germany, 30–33
    in India, 50–51
    ironmaking technology of, 154–55
    in Japan, 119
    minimills vs., 5, 33, 91, 92, 113–15
    productivity in, 114–15
    in Republic of Korea, 40–41
    scaling down, 142
    stagnation of, 184
    thin-slab casting adaptable to, 81
    U.S., 14, 19–23, 85–90, 105
International Iron and Steel Institute, 123, 129
Ipsco Inc., 27–28, 80
Iran, steel industry in, 10, 69, 70
Iretecna (formerly Italimpianti), 64
Iron and Steelmaker, 126
Iron carbide, 24, 153, 154, 185
Ironmaking process in steel mill of 21st century, 140, 153–56
Iron ore, 39, 144
ISCOR in South Africa, 22, 81, 154
ISPAT, 17, 67
Israel, steel industry in, 69, 70
Italy, steel industry in, 8, 9, 35–36, 76, 77, 79, 81, 84, 149
Ito Chu Corporation (formerly C. Itoh), 64, 68
Iverson, F. Kenneth, 173

Jacinto Group of the Philippines, 46
Japan, 2
    automotive industry in, 121, 122
    Direct Iron Ore Smelting (DIOS) Project, 150–51, 155, 156, 186

[Japan]
employment in, 9
exports and export market in, 9–10, 11, 72
future steel plans for, 9, 15–18, 72
integrated producers in, 119
joint ventures of, 64–65, 66, 68
minimills in, 16
overseas investments of, 17–18, 20, 47–48, 67, 95
raw materials preparation in, 150–51
steel construction in, 131
steel production and capacity (1980–1992), 12, 14
thin-slab casting in, 116, 117, 118–19
Japanese Economic Journal, 9
Japan Iron and Steel Federation, 18, 150, 156
Jindal Iron and Steel Company, 52
J&L, 88, 106
Joint ventures
Australian, 39, 40
in Brazil, 57
Chinese, 40, 44–45, 46
Japanese, 64–65, 66, 68
Korean, 43
in Taiwan, 62–63
in Thailand, 64–65
in U.S., 20, 22–23, 24, 25, 26
in Vietnam, 68

Kaiser Steel. *See* California Steel Company
Kawasaki Steel, 15, 22, 26, 47, 57, 58, 66, 119
Kazakhstan, 37
Klockner, 31–32, 155
Knoxville Iron, 75–76
Kobe Steel, 16, 17, 20, 65, 88
Korea. *See* Republic of Korea, steel industry in
Korean International Steel Associates, 40
Korf, Willy, 77, 158
Korf Group, 77
Krupp/Hoesch, 31, 32, 33
Krupp Industrietechnik, 178–79
Krupp Stahl, 62–63
Kwanwon Industries, 43
Kyoei Steel Works, 68

Laclede, 75, 106, 109
Ladle refining, 159–61
Lima Conference for Developing Countries (1975), 3, 8
Lion's Group, 65
Lloyd's Steel Industries, 52
Lone Star, 106
Low-end hot-strip mills, 108–9
LTV Steel, 21–22, 88, 105, 114–15, 155
Lumber in residential construction, 130, 132
Luxembourg, steel industry in, 34–35

Maanshan Steel Company, 48
McLouth, 105
Malayawata Steel, 67
Malaysia, 63, 65–67
Malaysian Iron and Steel Federation, 67
Mannesmann Demag Huttentechnik (MDH), 79, 117, 118, 167, 173
Manufacturing sector, ongoing revival of, 95
Marubeni, 17, 64, 65, 67
Mendoza, Cesar, 60
Metal Forming, 126
Mexico, steel industry in, 8, 11, 69
Middle East, steel industry in, 8, 69–70
Midrange hot-strip mills, 107–8
Midrex Direct Reduction Corporation, 153, 155
Minimills, 4–5, 74–119
in Australia, 38–39
in Brazil, 59
compact-strip technique of, 166, 167
competition between integrated mills and, 5, 33, 91, 92, 113–15
in Germany, 30–33
growth of, 184
impact of, from U.S. industry perspective, 14, 19, 24–28, 76–77, 79, 82–116
comparative cost trends, 113–15
flat-rolled demand through 2010, 98–101
flat-rolled demand vs. supply, 101–6

flat-rolled market, segments of,
106–9
increased competition, 90–92,
109–12
steel market outlook through
2010, 96–98
trends in U.S. steel demand,
92–96
U.S. industry restructuring,
85–90
in India, 53
in Indonesia, 67
in Japan, 16
as low-end market participants,
108–9
in Malaysia, 66
in People's Republic of China,
47–48
in Republic of Korea, 41–43
specialization of, 141–42
steel technology and, 75–77
in Thailand, 64
thin-slab casting and, 79–85
in Europe and Japan, 116–19
outlook for, 115–16
transformation of, 77–79
in United Kingdom, 29
Ministry of International Trade and
Industry, Science and Technology Agency Of (MITI), 18
Mitsubishi Chemicals, 151
Mitsui, 17, 64, 65, 67, 68
Monologue design concept, 125
Mung Development Company, 62
Myanmar Metal Industries, 43

National Association of Home Build-
ers, 132, 133
National Steel Company, 23, 105,
146, 152
Near-net-shape casting, 181–82
Netherlands, cokemaking capacity in,
149–50
New Jersey Steel, 110
Niche producers, 109
Nippon Steel, 15, 17, 22–23, 33, 34,
56, 63, 66, 67, 119
Nippon-Usiminas, 57
Nisshin, 16
Nisshio Iwai, 65
NKK, 15, 17, 18, 23, 64, 66, 67
Nomura Trading Company, 17, 64

Nonintegrated mills, capacity of, 105,
106. *See also* Minimills
North America, EC exports to, 72
North Korea, EC exports to, 72
North Star, 25, 84
Northwestern Steel & Wire, 5, 26, 75
NS Group, 80, 106, 109
Nucor, 5, 24, 26, 66, 79, 81, 91, 106,
109, 110, 113, 115, 117, 154,
157, 163, 165, 167
CSP plant, 165, 167, 168–73
thin-slab casting initiated by, 83–
84, 85
Nusantara Steel Corporation, 65, 67

Offgases, use of, 155, 157–58
Oil shock in 1970s, 2
Operating capacity, rate of, 13–14, 19
Oregon Steel, 25–26, 154
Overseas investment
Japanese, 17–18, 20, 47–48, 67, 95
Korean, 47

Pachura, Edmond, 123, 124, 127
Pakistan Steel, 68
Pennsylvania Steel Technologies, Inc.,
21
People's Republic of China, steel in-
dustry in, 4, 14, 72, 184
exports, 10–11
future steel plans of, 7–8, 43–48,
72, 73
joint ventures with, 40, 44–45, 46
Perwaja, 65–67
Peterson, Peter, 126–27
Plasma energy, 144
Plastics, use of, 5, 185
in appliance industry, 135–36, 137
in automotive industry, 121–28
Platzer high-reduction mill, 178, 179
Pohang Iron and Steel Company, 10,
20, 42, 162
Pollution, reducing, 185
Portman Mining, 40
POSCO, 26, 43, 81
Privatization of steel companies, 28,
37, 57, 58, 69, 96
Production, steel. *See* Steel production
Productivity, 95, 114–15, 159–60
Proler International, 110
Pulverized coal injection (PCI), 145–
49, 151–53, 186

Qatar, steel industry in, 69, 70
Qi Lu project, 46

Rationalization programs in U.S. steel
  companies, 87–88
Raw materials preparation, 140,
  144–53
  European Community (EC),
    147–50
  Japan, 150–51
  PCI outlook, 151–53
  United States, 145–47
Recession of 1970s, 2
Recyclability of steel vs. substitutes,
  127–28, 134
Reinforced concrete, 5, 128–29
Republic, 88
Republic of Korea, steel industry in, 8,
  10, 11, 12, 40–43, 47
Residential construction, steel used in,
  130–33
Residual alloys, 166
Restructuring of U.S. steel industry,
  85–90
Riva, 32, 33, 36, 118
Robotics, 141
Rolling technology, ongoing changes
  in, 182
Rouge Steel, 88, 105
Ruhrkohle, 147
Russia, steel industry in, 37–38

Sahaviriya Group, 64
SAIL, 50, 53
Sambrook, Gordon, 129
Sangkai Thai, 65
Saudi Arabia, steel industry in, 10, 69,
  70
Schloemann-Siemag (SMS), 79, 117,
  167, 180
  SMS Concast, 110, 167
Scrap loss, 3
Scrap usage, increasing, 142–43, 144,
  157
"Second-generation" mills, 105–6
Service-oriented economy, U.S., 93
Shanghai No. 3 Iron and Steel Com-
  pany, 43
Sheerness Steel Company, Ltd., 29, 157
Sheet steel product, 5
Shenyang Steel Rolling General Mill,
  47–48

Shenyang Toyo Steel, 47–48
Shougang Steel, 46
Siam Steel, 64
Siam Steel Pipe, 17
Siderbras, 59
Sidor, 69
Siemens of Germany, 39
Sino-Australian Channar Mine, 44–45
Sivensa, 69
Six-high cold mill, 182
Sollac, 123, 127
Somisa, 69
Southeast Asia, steel industry in, 17–
  18, 43, 63–68
South Korea. *See* Republic of Korea,
  steel industry in
Spain, steel industry in, 8, 9, 150
Specialization, 141–42
Steckel rolling mill, 180, 181
Steel industry
  employment in, 8, 9
  general trends in, 7–12, 71–73
  geographic location of, 3–4
  in post-World War II period, 1–4
  segments of world, v, 7
  in twenty-first century, changes
    in, 1
Steel market, state of, 89–90
Steel mill of the 21st century, 138–82
  finishing operations, 140, 181–82
  future advances in steel technology,
    v, 138–44
  ironmaking process, 140, 153–56
  major operating stages, 138–39,
    140
  raw materials preparation, 140,
    144–53
  steelmaking process, 140, 156–61
  thin-slab casting. *See under* Thin-
    slab casting
Steel production. *See also specific
  countries*
  in industrialized vs. developing
    countries, 183–84
  for 1974, 1980, and 1992, 8, 9
  post-World War II, 1–3
  total world production in 1992, 7
Substitute materials, 5–6, 93, 120–37,
  185
  in appliance industry, 120, 135–37
  in automotive industry, 5–6,
    120–28

in construction, 120, 128–33
in container industry, 130, 133–35
increased competition from, 91–92, 185
Sumitomo Metal Industries, 15–16, 17, 64

Tae Joon Park, 40
Taiwan, steel industry in, 8, 12, 61–63, 72
Tambascu, Marcus de Araujo, 58
Tang Eng, 62
Technology, advances in steel, v, 138–44. *See also* Steel mill of the 21st century
Tennessee Forging Steel Corporation, 76
Thai Coated Sheet Company, 17, 64, 65
Thailand, steel industry in, 63–65
Thai Siam Tinplate, 17
Thai Steel Pipe Company, 17, 64
Thai Wire, 17
Thin-slab casting, 5, 19
advent of, 110
in Europe and Japan, 116–19
minimills and, 79–85, 115–19
outlook for, 115–16
in People's Republic of China, 47–48
in steel mill of 21st century, 161–81
compact-strip outlook, 166–67
compact-strip production (CSP), 163, 168–73
compact vs. conventional, 161–63
concepts vs. reality, 163–65
in-line strip production (ISP), 163, 164, 165, 173–76
Krupp's ECCO mill, 178–79
quality considerations, 165–66, 167
thin-slab conticaster (TSC), 177–78
Thyssen's CPR process, 164, 165, 180
Tippin's TSP process, 180–81
VAI's Conroll process, 176–77
world capacity for, 82–83
Thin-slab conticaster (TSC), 177–78
Third world. *See* Developing countries

Thyssen Steel, 30–31, 32, 33, 117–18, 134, 147–48, 164, 165, 180
Tin-free steel, 133
Tinplate, 133, 134–35
Tippins Strip Process (TSP), 180–81
Toa Steel Company, 18
Tokyo Steel, 16–17, 80, 118, 119
Toyo Steel Manufacturing, 47–48
Transplants in U.S., 95, 96
Tuberao Steel Company (CST), 57, 58
Tung Ho, 62
Turkey, steel industry in, 8, 36–37, 118
Turkiye Demir ve Celik Islemeleri (TDCI), 118
Tuscaloosa, 106, 109

Ukraine, steel industry in, 37–38
Union Steel, 42
United Engineering Steels (UES), 29
United Kingdom, steel industry in, 9, 28–30, 129, 148
United States, steel industry in, 9, 18–28
automotive industry and, 121–28
capital expenditures by, 18–28
construction industry and, 128–33
employment in, 9
exports from developing countries to, 12
integrated companies, 14, 19–23, 85–90, 105
Japan's investments in, 17–18
joint ventures, 20, 22–23, 24, 25, 26
minimills in. *See under* Minimills
production and capacity (1980–1992), 12, 14
raw materials preparation in, 145–47
U.S. Department of Energy (DOE), 155–56
U.S. Export/Import Bank, 40, 56
United States Steel, 19–20, 81, 105, 110, 147
USS/Kobe, 88
USS/POSCO, 26
United States Steel Homes, 131
United Steelworkers Union, 114
Usiminas, 57, 59, 60, 69

Usinor Sacilor Steel Company, 30, 33–34, 117, 134, 148, 180
USSR, 37, 72
USX, 43
Uzbekistan, 37

Venezuela, steel industry in, 8, 69
Vietnam, steel industry in, 43, 68
Visakhaphenam (VIZAG), 51
Voest-Alpine Industrienlagenbau (VAI), 39, 52, 79, 154–55, 176–77

Ward's Automotive Yearbook for 1993, 127
Washington, 106
WCI, 88
Wei Chi Steel Industries, 18

Weirton Steel, 23, 88, 105, 134
Werner, Jeffry, 79
Western Australian-China Economic and Technology Research Fund, 44
Westinghouse, 170
Wheeling-Pittsburgh, 23
World Bank, 40
World steel capacity, 1–2, 4
Worthington Corporation, 20

Yamato Kogyo, 64
Yamato Steel, 5, 16, 24, 118–19
Yieh Loong Steel Group, 62
Yield loss, 102

Zhanjang project, 45

About the Author

William T. Hogan, S.J., was graduated from Fordham College cum laude and received his M.A. and Ph.D. in Economics from Fordham University. He is currently Professor of Economics and Director of the Industrial Economics Research Institute at Fordham University.

Father Hogan has been engaged in economic studies of the steel industry and other basic, heavy industries for over 35 years. During this time, he has authored a number of books, among which are *Productivity in the Blast Furnace and Open-Hearth Segments of the Steel Industry*, the first detailed study on the subject of steel productivity, and *The Development of Heavy Industry in the Twentieth Century*. In 1967, *Depreciation Policies and Resultant Problems* was published.

His landmark, five-volume work, *Economic History of the Iron and Steel Industry in the United States*, covering industry developments from 1860 to 1971, was published by the Lexington Books Division of D.C. Heath and Company in 1971. This was followed by the first of its companion studies, *The 1970s: Critical Years for Steel,* which was published in 1972. In 1982, his book entitled *World Steel in the 1980s: A Case of Survival* was published. These works were followed by *Steel in the United States, Restructuring to Compete*, published in 1984, *Minimills and Integrated Mills: A Comparison of Steelmaking in the United States*, published in 1987, and *Global Steel in the 1990s: Growth or Decline*, which was published in 1990. His book, *Capital Investment in Steel: A World Plan for the 1990s*, was published in September 1992.

In 1950, Father Hogan inaugurated the Industrial Economics Research Institute at Fordham University, which has produced studies dealing with economic problems of an industrial nature.

He has appeared before legislative committees of both the United States Senate and the House of Representatives and has testified on many occasions before the Ways and Means Committee of the House of Representatives on

201

legislation affecting depreciation charges and capital investment. He has also appeared before the Finance Committee of the Senate to testify on tax incentives for capital spending. He served as a member of the Presidential Task Force on Business Taxation and was a consultant to the Council of Economic Advisors to the President and the U.S. Department of Commerce.

During the past 25 years, Father Hogan has visited most of the steel-producing facilities in the world and has delivered papers at steel conferences in the United States, Great Britain, France, Sweden, Switzerland, Czechoslovakia, Russia, Venezuela, Brazil, South Africa, India, the Philippines, Japan, and South Korea.

In 1985, Father Hogan was awarded the Gary Memorial Medal by the American Iron and Steel Institute. This is the highest honor that the steel industry can bestow. In 1987, he was given a Distinguished Life Membership by the American Society of Metals (ASM) International, and in 1990, the William T. Hogan, S.J., Annual Lecture Series was established in his honor by the Association of Iron and Steel Engineers.

In October of 1992, he was honored by the Republic of Korea when President Roh Tae-woo presented him with the prestigious Gold Tower of the Order of Industrial Merit, the highest award given in business by the government. In 1993, at its Paris, France meeting, the International Iron and Steel Institute (IISI) made Father Hogan an Honorary Member. The IISI has an international membership of most of the steel companies in the world. In its twenty-seven-year history, there are only two honorary members, of which Father Hogan is the second.